A NURSERY RHYME FOR EVERY NIGHT OF THE YEAR

Also by Allie Esiri
and available from Macmillan

A Poem for Every Night of the Year

A Poem for Every Day of the Year

A Poem for Every Autumn Day

A Poem for Every Winter Day

A Poem for Every Spring Day

A Poem for Every Summer Day

A Poet for Every Day of the Year

Shakespeare for Every Day of the Year

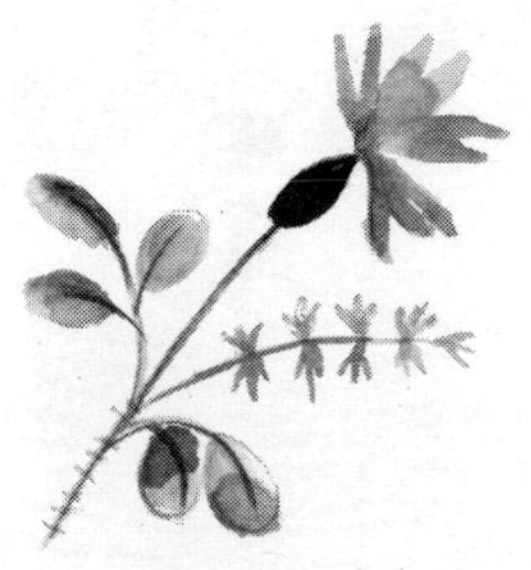

A NURSERY RHYME FOR EVERY NIGHT OF THE YEAR

One of a limited signed edition

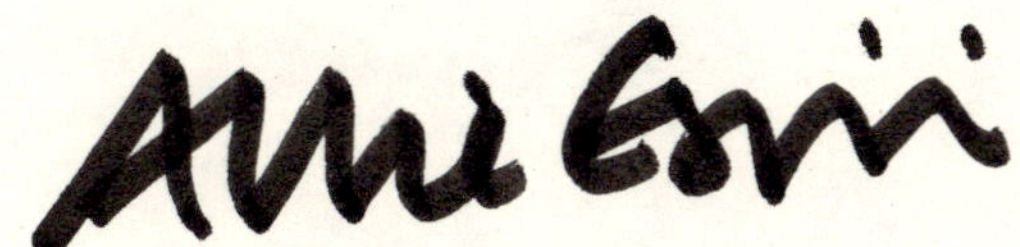

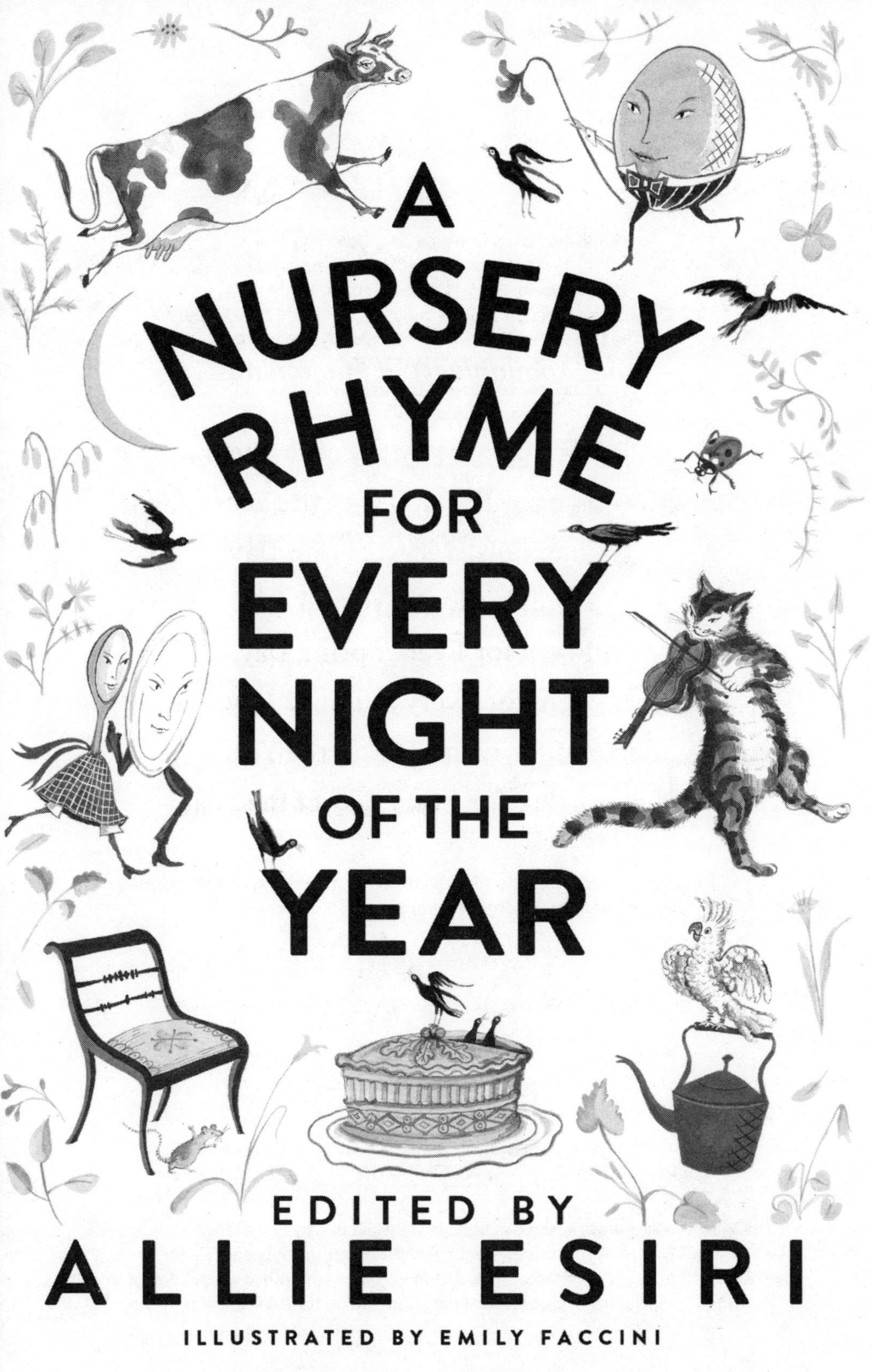

A NURSERY RHYME FOR EVERY NIGHT OF THE YEAR

EDITED BY

ALLIE ESIRI

ILLUSTRATED BY EMILY FACCINI

MACMILLAN CHILDREN'S BOOKS

Published 2023 by Macmillan Children's Books
an imprint of Pan Macmillan
The Smithson, 6 Briset Street, London EC1M 5NR
EU representative: Macmillan Publishers Ireland Ltd, 1st Floor,
The Liffey Trust Centre, 117–126 Sheriff Street Upper
Dublin 1, D01 YC43
Associated companies throughout the world
www.panmacmillan.com

ISBN 978-1-0350-1332-6

1 3 5 7 9 8 6 4 2

A CIP catalogue record for this book is available from the British Library.

Printed and bound by CPI Group (UK) Ltd, Croydon CR0 4YY

To my mother and father – thank you!

Contents

February: Love, Pancake Day

March: Spring, Women's Day, Riddles

April: April Fool's Day, Spring Festivals, Tongue Twisters

May: May Day, Farm, Market, London

June: Playground Games, Animals

July: Weather Lore, Travel, Classics

August: Sea, Rivers, Outdoors

September: Back to School

October: Food, Action Songs, Halloween

November: History, Divali, Thanksgiving

December: Lullabies, Festive Rhymes

'Tell it again, tell it the same.'

Is 'Humpty Dumpty' Richard III falling off his horse at the Battle of Bosworth, a cautionary metaphor for falling from a great height, or just an unlucky egg? There is a plethora of interpretations for every nursery rhyme, but each tends to defy theory and live on regardless, handed down happily from generation to generation.

Inside these pages are 366 nursery rhymes, one for every night of the year. The great classics sit alongside more contemporary rhymes, with some – thanks to present-day poets – even composed especially for this anthology. Daily introductions cover historical facts or quirky anecdotes, answers to riddles and actions for songs, with magnificent illustrations by Emily Faccini.

What is a nursery rhyme? The term, first recorded in 1816, is defined by the *Oxford English Dictionary* as 'a simple or traditional poem or song for children'. They tend to be short and easy to remember, and couldn't really be more full of rhythm, rhyme and repetition. The archetype of poetry, they are preserved by an oral tradition, traditionally sung at home or in a market square by a balladeer to a population that would have been largely illiterate, just as we are when first hearing them, at the age before we can read, write or even talk.

The writer Vita Sackville-West said of nursery rhymes that they lead children (who can talk) to insist, 'Tell it again, tell it the same.' However, this very characteristic of constant recitation is precisely how small changes have crept in over time, and these small adaptations are key to their immortality.

Despite being mainly orally reproduced, this hasn't stopped us anthologists from trying to capture them like pressed flowers. While there is evidence in historic plays (among other sources) that nursery rhymes were being sung and spoken long before, the first collection seems not to have been printed until *Tommy Thumb's Pretty Song Book* appeared in 1744. Then in 1781 *Mother Goose's Melody: or Sonnets for the Cradle* became a publishing sensation, leading to a 1785 reprint in the United States. Mother Goose's name is still associated with the gathering of rhymes today, although there is no evidence that any such historical figure ever existed. The name first appeared in France in Charles Perrault's early eighteenth-century anthology of fairy tales, *Les Contes de ma mère l'Oye*, whose translation for the English-speaking world was *Tales of Mother Goose*.

Nursery rhymes can be whimsical or strictly didactic, and take a variety of forms, including limericks, tongue-twisters, skipping rhymes, story ballads, alphabet songs and lullabies. Many are utterly beautiful – the poet Robert Graves said the best of nursery rhymes are nearer to poetry than the greater part of *The Oxford Book of English Verse*. Learned within the safe confines of home, there are myriad themes with allegorical meanings or a warning: from Humpty Dumpty's fall to the old man who bumped his head, or the baby who fell out of the cradle. If the meaning or warning is complex or dark, it tends only to reveal itself later in life.

Many have recognized their worth, and as you will discover in this book, they continue to be an inspiration for artists such as Paula Rego, lyricists like Rihanna and Taylor Swift, and football fans who constantly adapt them to chant on the terraces.

I hope you enjoy sharing these nursery rhymes. And when you are ready, do try the next book in the series, *A Poem for Every Night of the Year*. After all, a poem is just a nursery rhyme that has grown up.

Allie Esiri

JANUARY

Winter, Bedtime

1 January • I Saw Three Ships Come Sailing By • Anon.

Happy New Year! Nursery rhymes tend to change over time as they are passed down the generations in an oral tradition. This New Year's Day ditty is no exception – there is an alternative version that you could choose to recite in December as it has the three ships come sailing by on 'Christmas Day in the morning'.

I saw three ships come sailing by,
Come sailing by, come sailing by;
I saw three ships come sailing by,
On New Year's Day in the morning.

And what do you think was in them then,
Was in them then, was in them then?
And what do you think was in them then,
On New Year's Day in the morning?

Three pretty girls were in them then,
Were in them then, were in them then;
Three pretty girls were in them then,
On New Year's Day in the morning.

And one could whistle, and one could sing,
And one could play the violin –
Such joy there was at my wedding,
On New Year's Day in the morning.

2 January • The North Wind Doth Blow • Anon.

Across the world, a northerly wind means bad news. While Australians might associate the north wind with bushfires, for the Northern Hemisphere a north wind signals incoming harsh, cold weather, as suffered by the creatures in this poem. Aside from being a staple favourite, this rhyme has introduced generations of children to animal migration and hibernation. The folk singer Carole King's 1971 song, and *Toy Story* hit, 'You've Got a Friend' references this classic rhyme, with the line 'And that old north wind begins to blow' as a marker of hard times.

The north wind doth blow,
And we shall have snow,
And what will poor robin do then,
  Poor thing?
He'll sit in a barn,
And keep himself warm,
And hide his head under his wing.
  Poor thing!

The north wind doth blow,
And we shall have snow,
And what will the swallow do then,
  Poor thing?
Oh, do you not know
That he's off long ago
To a country where he will find spring,
  Poor thing!

The north wind doth blow,
And we shall have snow,
And what will the dormouse do then,
  Poor thing?
Rolled up like a ball
In his nest snug and small,
He'll sleep till warm weather comes in,
  Poor thing!

The north wind doth blow,
And we shall have snow,
And what will the honey-bee do then,
  Poor thing?
In his hive he will stay
Till the cold is away,
And then he'll come out in the spring,
  Poor thing!

The north wind doth blow,
And we shall have snow,
And what will the children do then,
  Poor things?
When lessons are done
They will skip, jump and run
Until they have made themselves warm,
  Poor things!

3 January • There Once Was a Man Named Michael Finnegan • Anon.

First noted in 1921, this Irish rhyme is a close relative to other classic nursery rhymes, with the joke of futility at its core recognizable from many others – see, for instance, 'The Grand Old Duke of York' (15 November). As befits a rhyme that ends where it begins, it is referenced, along with other nursery rhymes, in James Joyce's famously baffling novel *Finnegans Wake* (which does the same thing): 'such is manowife's lot of lose and win again, like he's gruen quhiskers on who's chin again, she plucketed them out but they grown in again' [sic].

There once was a man named Michael Finnegan,
He grew whiskers on his chin-igan,
The wind came up and blew them in again,
Poor old Michael Finnegan. Begin again!

There once was a man named Michael Finnegan,
He kicked up an awful din-igan
Because they said he must not sing again,
Poor old Michael Finnegan. Begin again.

There once was a man named Michael Finnegan,
Ran a race and tried to win again,
Got so puffed that he had to go in again,
Poor old Michael Finnegan. Begin again.

There once was a man named Michael Finnegan,
He drank through all his good gin again,
And so he wasted all his tin again,
Poor old Michael Finnegan. Begin again.

There once was a man named Michael Finnegan,
He went fishing with a pin again,
He caught a fish but dropped it in again,
Poor old Michael Finnegan. Begin again.

There once was a man named Michael Finnegan,
Climbed a tree and barked his shin-igan,
Took off several yards of skin-igan,
Poor old Michael Finnegan. Begin again.

There once was a man named Michael Finnegan,
He grew fat and then grew thin again.
Poor old Michael Finnegan. Begin again!

4 January • Beans • Michael Rosen

Let's begin again, with the contemporary poet Michael Rosen's whimsical piece about a downpouring of baked beans. Given what we know from another childhood rhyme beginning 'Beans, beans, good for your heart . . . ', it is not so much the rain we might worry about, but the wind.

It's bad out there
It's scary, it's weird
You thought it was hard
But it's worse than you feared.

Next time they say it'll be 'cloudy'
Do you know what that really means?
Yes, of course it's going to rain
But it's going to rain baked beans.

Millions and millions of beans
Are going to fall out of the sky
All over me and you
I promise you this is no lie.

The streets will be covered with beans,
Over houses and cars and vans.
Your hair will be sticky with beans,
There'll be beans all over your hands.

Towers will drip with the juice.
Houses will all disappear.
It's going to be something that lasts
For anything up to a year.

Bulldozers will be called into action,
They'll try to move the muck,
But after just a few minutes
Most of them will be stuck.

People will go out with hoses,
Buckets, jugs and cups,
And hundreds of hungry people
Will try to gobble it up.

It'll take ten years in all
To clean up every little bean.
So remember – next time you hear the word 'cloudy'
You know what it will mean.

5 January • It's Raining, It's Pouring • Anon.

Children delight in rhymes about the rain, although sensible grown-ups have long been concerned by this old man's head injury!

> It's raining, it's pouring,
> The old man is snoring,
> He went to bed and bumped his head,
> And couldn't get up in the morning.

6 January • Rain, Will You Come Today? • Brian Bilston

The classic imploring lines 'Rain, rain, go away, / Come again another day', repeated so often at British summer barbecues, has been rewritten many times, with variants dating back to Ancient Greece. Yet the pseudonymous poet Brian Bilston (aka 'the Banksy of Poetry') here turns this saying on its head.

> Rain, will you come today?
> Make the skies turn dark and grey
> Please come quick, I think you should –
> I want to play out in the mud
>
> Rain, will you come today?
> Tip down now – please don't delay!
> I'd be really grateful if you could
> I want mud pie for my pud

Hop it, sunshine, on your way
The rain is coming down. Hooray!
Big, fat raindrops feel so good
Mmm . . . thick and gloopy, lovely mud!

7 January • If All Were Rain and Never Sun • Christina Rossetti

The great Victorian poet Christina Rossetti (1830–1894) wrote this sweet poem for *Sing-Song,* her collection of rhymes for the nursery.

If all were rain and never sun,
No bow could span the hill;
If all were sun and never rain,
There'd be no rainbow still.

8 January • I Hear Thunder, I Hear Thunder • Anon.

Sung to the tune and following the structure of 'Frère Jacques', today's entry also touches on the fun that rain represents for many children.

I hear thunder, I hear thunder,
Hark don't you, hark don't you?
    Pitter patter raindrops
    Pitter patter raindrops,
I'm wet through, so are you.

9 January • The Fox Went Out on a Chilly Night • Anon.

This traditional narrative rhyme, dating back to the nineteenth century, exists in alternative forms across England and America, but all with similarly grisly outcomes, long enjoyed by children.

The fox went out on a chilly night,
He prayed to the moon to give him light,
For he'd many a mile to go that night
Before he reached the town-o, town-o, town-o,
He had many a mile to go that night
Before he reached the town-o.

He ran till he came to a great big bin
Where the ducks and the geese were put therein.
'A couple of you will grease my chin
Before I leave this town-o, town-o, town-o,
A couple of you will grease my chin
Before I leave this town-o.'

He grabbed the grey goose by the neck,
Threw the grey goose behind his back;
He didn't mind their quack, quack, quack,
And their legs all a-dangling down-o, down-o, down-o,
He didn't mind their quack, quack, quack,
And their legs all a-dangling down-o.

Old Mother pitter patter jumped out of bed;
Out of the window she cocked her head,
Crying, 'John, John! The grey goose is gone

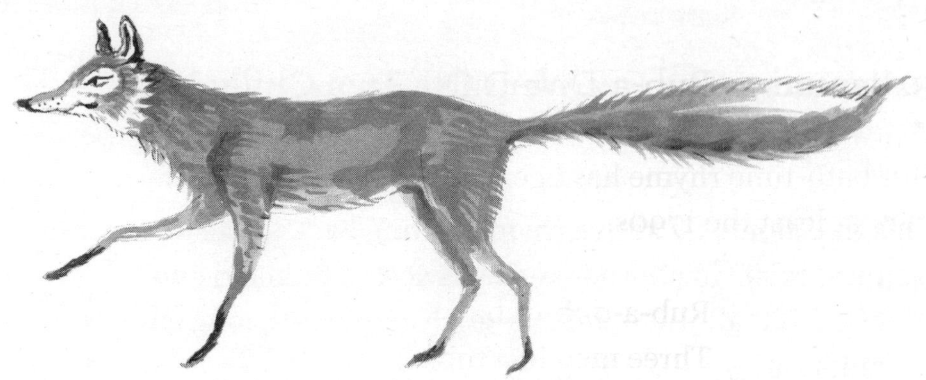

And the fox is on the town-o, town-o, town-o!'
Crying, 'John, John, the grey goose is gone
and the fox is on the town-o!'

Then John he went to the top of the hill,
Blew his horn both loud and shrill;
The fox he said, 'I'd better flee with my kill,
He'll soon be on my trail-o, trail-o, trail-o.'
The fox he said, 'I'd better flee with my kill,
He'll soon be on my trail-o.'

He ran till he came to his cosy den;
There were the little ones, eight, nine, ten.
They said, 'Daddy, better go back again,
'Cause it must be a mighty fine town-o, town-o, town-o!'
They said, 'Daddy, better go back again,
'Cause it must be a mighty fine town-o.'

Then the fox and his wife without any strife
Cut up the goose with a fork and knife.
They never had such a supper in their life,
And the little ones chewed on the bones-o, bones-o, bones-o,
They never had such a supper in their life,
And the little ones chewed on the bones-o.

10 January • Rub-a-Dub-Dub • Anon.

This bath-time rhyme has been around, in its various forms, since at least the 1790s.

Rub-a-dub-dub,
Three men in a tub:
And who do you think they be?
The butcher, the baker,
The candlestick-maker,
And all of them out to sea.

11 January • Anthony Washes • E. V. Rieu

Fans of ancient classics may be surprised to learn that E. V. Rieu, renowned for his translation of Homer's *Odyssey,* also wrote this delightful poem for children.

Anthony washed his face today –
Nobody made him do it:
He wasn't helped in the usual way;
Nobody helped him through it.

Anthony, Anthony, are you ill?
Or is my eyesight failing?
You've washed your face of your own free will –
Anthony, are you ailing?

12 January • Good Night, Sleep Tight • Anon

There are many variants of this little bedtime rhyme. The most popular consists of just the first two lines, others replace 'bed-bugs' with 'mosquitoes', and a bug-free version is 'Good night, sleep tight, wake up bright in the morning light.'

Good night, sleep tight,
Don't let the bed-bugs bite.
If they bite, squeeze them tight,
Then they won't bite another night.

13 January • *from* Night • William Blake

If the previous rhymes helped to get you ready for bed, this lullaby might get you off to sleep. It is extracted from Romantic poet William Blake's (1757–1827) illustrated poem 'Night', one of his *Songs of Innocence* (1789).

The sun descending in the west,
The evening star does shine;
The birds are silent in their nest,
And I must seek for mine.
The moon like a flower
In heaven's high bower,
With silent delight
Sits and smiles on the night.

14 January • One More Story • Julia Donaldson

More recently Julia Donaldson, beloved author of *The Gruffalo* (1999), gave us this bedtime rhyme.

One more story – you've only told me one.
Tell me the one about the runaway bun!
How about the dragon who never learnt to roar?
One more story – just one more!

One more story – you've only told me two.
Tell me the one about the dinosaur poo!
How about the monster behind the secret door?
One more story – just one more!

One more story – you've only told me three.
Tell me the one about the champion flea!
How about a story I've never heard before?
One more story – just one more!

Why aren't you answering? Did I hear you snore?

15 January • Bed is Too Small for my Tiredness • Anon.

These quatrains (verses of four lines) were popularized by Girl Guide groups who sang them as a campfire lullaby throughout the twentieth century.

Bed is too small for my tiredness,
Give me a hilltop with trees.
Tuck a cloud up under my chin,
Lord blow the moon out, please.

Rock me to sleep in a cradle of dreams,
Send me a lullaby of leaves.
Tuck a cloud up under my chin,
Lord blow the moon out, please.

16 January • Wee Willie Winkie • William Miller

This famous nursery rhyme was written by the nineteenth-century Scottish poet William Miller (1810–72). Some attempts have been made to relate the character 'Willie Winkie' to William III (1650–1702), as it was one of the king's nicknames – though you would have been pretty brave to use it if you'd met him!

Wee Willie Winkie runs through the town,
Upstairs and downstairs in his nightgown,
Rapping at the window, crying through the lock,
'Are the children in their beds, for now it's eight o'clock?'

17 January • Vespers • A. A. Milne

The following bedtime rhyme is from A. A. Milne, the beloved creator of Winnie-the-Pooh. Christopher Robin, whom you'll remember from the *Pooh* books, was the name of Milne's son, (who spent his life mortified by what he called the 'toe-curling, fist-clenching, lip-biting embarrassment' of his fictional fame).

Little Boy kneels at the foot of the bed,
Droops on the little hands little gold head.
Hush! Hush! Whisper who dares!
Christopher Robin is saying his prayers

God bless Mummy. I know that's right.
Wasn't it fun in the bath to-night?
The cold's so cold, and the hot's so hot.
Oh! God bless Daddy – I quite forgot.

If I open my fingers a little bit more,
I can see Nanny's dressing-gown on the door.
It's a beautiful blue, but it hasn't a hood.
Oh! God bless Nanny and make her good.

Mine has a hood, and I lie in bed,
And pull the hood right over my head,
And I shut my eyes, and I curl up small,
And nobody knows that I'm there at all.

Oh! Thank you, God, for a lovely day.
And what was the other I had to say?
I said 'Bless Daddy,' so what can it be?
Oh! Now I remember it. God bless Me.

Little Boy kneels at the foot of the bed,
Droops on the little hands little gold head.
Hush! Hush! Whisper who dares!
Christopher Robin is saying his prayers.

18 January • Kumbaya • Anon.

'Kumbaya' emerged during the dark times of American slavery as an appeal for God to 'come by here' and help. 'Kumbaya' is the rendering of this phrase in Gullah, a Creole language. A famous recording of Civil Rights marchers singing it on their way from Selma to Montgomery in 1965 helped cement its association with the Civil Rights Movement. As Martin Luther King Jr. (1929–1968) was one of the leaders of these marches, 'Kumbaya' is a fitting entry for Martin Luther King Jr. Day, which falls on the third Monday of January.

Kumbaya, my Lord, Kumbaya;
Kumbaya, my Lord, Kumbaya;
Kumbaya, my Lord, Kumbaya,
O Lord, Kumbaya.

Someone's laughing, my Lord, Kumbaya;
Someone's laughing, my Lord, Kumbaya;
Someone's laughing, my Lord, Kumbaya;
O Lord, Kumbaya.

Someone's crying, my Lord, Kumbaya;
Someone's crying, my Lord, Kumbaya;
Someone's crying, my Lord, Kumbaya;
O Lord, Kumbaya.

Someone's praying, my Lord, Kumbaya;
Someone's praying, my Lord, Kumbaya;
Someone's praying, my Lord, Kumbaya;
O Lord, Kumbaya.

19 January • Matthew, Mark, Luke and John • Anon.

Variants of this pious bedtime rhyme can be found all over Europe. It is another that James Joyce uses in *Finnegans Wake*, parodying the Evangelists as 'Mildew, murk, leak and yarn'. Incidentally, in the Bible, each of the Evangelists has a symbolic animal associated with them: Matthew (winged man, or angel); Mark (lion); Luke (ox); and John (eagle) – hence 'two to bear my soul away' are the two with wings.

Matthew, Mark, Luke, and John,
Bless the bed that I lie on.
Four corners to my bed,
Four angels round my head;
One to watch and one to pray,
And two to bear my soul away.

20 January • Bye, Baby Bunting • Anon.

'Baby bunting' is an old-fashioned term of endearment, popular in the eighteenth century.

Bye, baby bunting,
Daddy's gone a-hunting,
Gone to get a rabbit skin
To wrap the baby bunting in.

21 January • Here's a Body – There's a Bed! • Anon.

Considering how nursery rhymes change over time, we might wonder whether the last line's 'puff' of a candle being blown out might soon be replaced with the 'click' of a light-switch . . . or even, 'Alexa, OFF!'

Here's a body – there's a bed!
There's a pillow – here's a head!
There's a curtain – here's a light!
There's a puff – and so goodnight!

22 January • Star Light, Star Bright • Anon.

This simple bedtime rhyme has had a glittering music career, having been recycled in Joni Mitchell's 1971 song 'This Flight Tonight', and sung by the Queen of Pop, Madonna, as a refrain in her 1983 hit 'Lucky Star'.

Star light, star bright,
First star I see tonight,
I wish I may, I wish I might,
Have the wish I wish tonight.

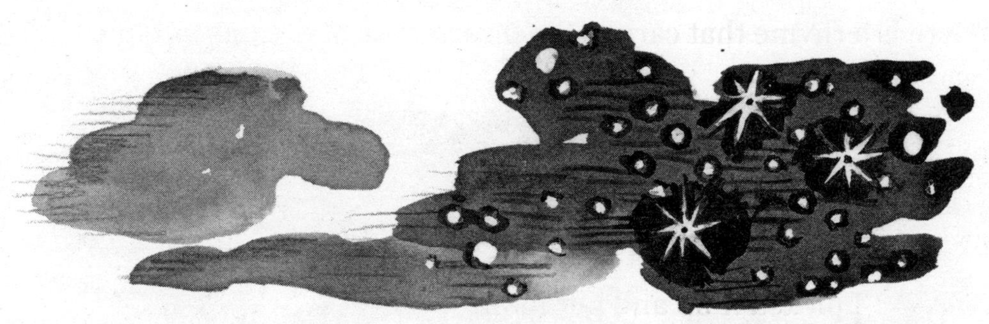

23 January • If You Hear • Clare Bevan

Clare Bevan is a poet writing for young children today, whose favourite themes include magic and fairies.

If you think you hear a rustle
In the grasses by your door,
If you spot a tiny footprint

In the dust upon your floor,
If you see a baby sleeping
In the petals of a rose,
If you peer inside a mouse hole
And a lantern softly glows,
If your tooth, so small and precious,
Is collected in the night,
Then perhaps you'll find the doorway
To the magic Land of Light.

24 January • As I Was Going Out One Day • Anon.

Here is a rhyme that carries the bizarreness of dreams into the waking world.

As I was going out one day,
My head fell off and ran away.
But when I saw that it was gone,
I picked it up and put it on.

And when I got into the street,
A fellow cried: 'LOOK AT YOUR FEET!'
I looked at him and sadly said:
'I'VE LEFT THEM BOTH ASLEEP IN BED!'

25 January • Diddle, Diddle, Dumpling, my Son John • Anon.

The refrain 'Diddle, diddle, dumpling' in this rhyme originates from a street cry that used to be common among English sellers of hot dumplings. The rhyme dates back to at least the eighteenth century.

Diddle, diddle, dumpling, my son John,
Went to bed with his trousers on;
One shoe off, one shoe on,
Diddle, diddle, dumpling, my son John.

26 January • A Bedtime Rhyme for Young Fairies • Clare Bevan

Here is another delightful rhyme for bedtime by Clare Bevan.

One tired fairy,
Two folded wings,
Three magic wishes,
Four daisy rings,
Five moonlight dancers,
Six starlight spells,
Seven hidden treasures,
Eight silver bells,
Nine secret doorways,
Ten keys to keep,
And one little fairy
Fast asleep.

27 January • Hey Diddle Diddle • Anon.

Today's entry is perhaps the best-known example of English nonsense. Two writers of fantasy novels, the *Lord of the Rings* author J. R. R. Tolkien and *Wizard of Oz* writer L. Frank Baum, have had fun with it in their books.

Hey diddle diddle,
The cat and the fiddle,
The cow jumped over the moon;
The little dog laughed
To see such sport,
And the dish ran away with the spoon.

28 January • The Man in the Moon • Anon.

Like the last rhyme, this lunar ditty has made its mark on literature, even finding its way into a letter by Mrs Micawber in Charles Dickens's *David Copperfield* (1850).

The man in the moon
Came tumbling down,
And asked his way to Norwich;
He went by the south,
And burnt his mouth,
With supping cold pease-porridge.

29 January • I Dreamed that my Horse had Wings and Could Fly • Anon.

To end our run of night-time rhymes, we have this dream metamorphosis from common nag to flying horse.

I dreamed that my horse had wings and could fly,
I jumped on my horse and rode to the sky.
The man in the moon was out that night,
He laughed long and loud when I pranced into sight.

30 January • The Animals All Swam in the Race • Anon.

Chinese New Year usually falls around the end of January in our modern (Gregorian) calendar. Each year is associated with one of twelve animals. Legend has it that these animals had a race to determine their place in the cycle, crossing the finishing line as follows: rat; ox; tiger; rabbit; dragon; snake; horse; sheep; monkey; rooster; dog; pig.

The animals all swam in the race,
The animals all swam in the race,
The animals all swam in the race,
Are you ready steady go?

The ox was strong and he swam very fast,
The ox was strong and he swam very fast,
The ox was strong and he swam very fast,
And he thought he'd won the race.

The clever little rat jumped onto his tail,
The clever little rat jumped onto his back,
The clever little rat jumped over his head,
And the rat won the race instead.

The rat came first and the pig came last,
The rat came first and the pig came last,
The rat came first and the pig came last,
And that was the end of the race.

31 January • Can You Hear the Dragon, the Dragon, the Dragon? • Anon.

The traditional festivities associated with Chinese New Year include 'dragon dances', which are performed to ward off evil spirits.

Can you hear the dragon, the dragon, the dragon?
Can you hear the dragon? His roar is very loud.
Can you hear the dragon, the dragon, the dragon?
Can you hear the dragon? He's coming through the crowd.

Can you see the dragon, the dragon, the dragon?
Can you see the dragon? He's dancing in the street.
Can you see the dragon, the dragon, the dragon?
Can you see the dragon? He has claws upon his feet.

Can you see the dragon, the dragon, the dragon?
Can you see the dragon? His tail is very long.
Can you see the dragon, the dragon, the dragon?
Can you see the dragon? His teeth are very strong.

Can you see the dragon, the dragon, the dragon?
Can you see the dragon? There's fire in his breath.
Can you see the dragon, the dragon, the dragon?
Can you see the dragon? He'll frighten you to death.

February

Love, Pancake Day

1 February • Roses are Red • Anon.

February is a month for love, in all its forms. Today's entry might be the most ubiquitous love poem of all. Its earliest variant appeared over four hundred years ago, in Elizabethan England, as a very small part of the epic poem *The Faerie Queene* by Edmund Spenser (c. 1553–1599): 'She bath'd with roses red, and violets blew, / And all the sweetest flowres, that in the forrest grew'. Recent playful versions include, 'Roses are red, violets are blue, poetry is hard. Avocado'.

Roses are red,
Violets are blue,
Sugar is sweet,
And so are you.

2 February • Chillies are Red • Smriti Halls

Today's entry is a brand-new response to the 'Roses are red' rhyme, especially written for us by the acclaimed children's writer Smriti Halls.

Chillies are red,
Peacocks are blue,
Jasmine is sweet,
And so are you.

. . . But chillies can *burn*,
Some jasmine's *too* sweet,
And peacocks can *peck* . . .
Be fast on your feet!

3 February • Skid-a-ma-rink • Felix F. Feist

During the Tin Pan Alley era, when almost all popular American songs seemed to originate in a single district of New York, Felix F. Feist (1883–1936) wrote these lyrics for a Broadway musical in 1910.

Skid-a-ma-rink, a-dink a-dink,
Skid-a-ma-rink a-doo.
    I love you!
Skid-a-ma-rink, a-dink a-dink,
Skid-a-ma-rink a-doo.
    I love you!
I love you in the morning,
And in the afternoon.

I love you in the evening,
And underneath the moon.
Oh skid-a-ma-rink, a-dink a-dink a-dink,
Skid-a-marink a-doo.
        I love you!

4 February • Blow a Kiss • Joseph Coelho

This new nursery rhyme is by the writer and performance poet Joseph Coelho, the the current UK Children's Laureate.

Blow a kiss,
Catch a kiss
When we are apart.

Blow a kiss,
Catch a kiss
Put it in your heart.

5 February • Tinker, Tailor, Soldier, Sailor • Anon.

Nursery rhymes often turn the complex business of love into delightfully simple games. This fortune-telling one, which is usually recited whilst counting out flower petals or cherry stones. You'll find variants all over the place. In Scotland we have 'A laird, a lord, / A cooper, a thief, / A piper, a drummer / A stealer of beef', while in America it's 'Rich man, poor man, beggarman, thief, / Doctor, lawyer, merchant, chief'. Otherwise, for picking female partners (albeit from a dismayingly limited range of career options), you might have recited 'Rich girl, poor girl, beggar, crook / Schoolgirl, phone girl, servant girl, cook'.

Tinker,
    Tailor,
Soldier,
    Sailor,
Rich man,
    Poor man,
Beggarman,
    Thief.

6 February • A Tisket, a Tasket • Anon.

These fabulous lines were rendered into a jaunty tune by Ella Fitzgerald and Chick Webb for the 1938 mega-hit 'A-Tisket, A-Tasket' – the song widely credited for Fitzgerald's meteoric rise to fame. The rhyme also forms the basis of a circle singing game. One child skips around the circle carrying a basket with a folded letter in it. At the end of the song, the child stops and places the letter behind one of the seated children. This child then stands and picks up the letter, and they both chase around the circle in opposite directions to race back to the vacant space.

A tisket, a tasket,
A green and yellow basket.
I wrote a letter to my love,
But on the way I dropped it.
I dropped it, I dropped it,
And on the way, I dropped it.
A little boy picked it up,
And put it in his pocket.

7 February • Rig-a-Jig-Jig • Anon.

Rig-a-Jig-Jig is a children's circle game known since the nineteenth century. One player is nominated as the 'young man', while the rest are arranged in a circle of 'pretty ladies'. The young man stands in the middle and sings the first three lines; on 'I chanced to meet', the young man bows to a ‘pretty lady’, and they join hands to sing the chorus together, moving in and out of the circle. Another player from the circle becomes the new ‘young man’ and this process repeats until all players are partnered.

> As I was walking down the street,
> Heigh ho, heigh ho, heigh ho, heigh ho,
> A pretty lady [*or* nice young man] I chanced to meet,
> Heigh ho, heigh ho, heigh ho, heigh ho.
> Rig-a-jig-jig and away we go, away we go, away we go,
> Rig-a-jig-jig and away we go,
> Heigh ho, heigh ho, heigh ho, heigh ho.

8 February • Oh, Where Have You Been, Billy Boy, Billy Boy? • Anon.

This British ballad from the eighteenth or nineteenth century became very popular in America, and continues to inspire musicians and filmmakers alike. In 1941 Pete Seeger and Lee Hays turned it into an anti-war protest song, Miles Davis reworked it as a key modern jazz piece of the 1950s, and it provided the title for the 1983 New York film *Can She Bake a Cherry Pie?*.

Oh, where have you been, Billy Boy, Billy Boy,
    Oh, where have you been, charming Billy?
I have been to seek a wife, she’s the joy of my life,
    She’s a young thing and cannot leave her mother.

Did she ask you to come in, Billy Boy, Billy Boy,
    Did she ask you to come in, charming Billy?
Yes, she asked me to come in, there's a dimple in her chin.
    She's a young thing and cannot leave her mother.

Can she make a cherry pie, Billy Boy, Billy Boy,
    Can she make a cherry pie, charming Billy?
She can make a cherry pie, quick as a cat can wink an eye,
    She's a young thing and cannot leave her mother.

Can she make a feather bed, Billy Boy, Billy Boy?
    Can she make a feather bed, charming Billy?
She can make a feather bed and put pillows at the head,
    She's a young thing and cannot leave her mother.

How tall is she, Billy Boy, Billy Boy?
    How tall is she, charming Billy?
She's as tall as a pine, and straight as a pumpkin vine,
    She's a young thing and cannot leave her mother.

How old is she, Billy Boy, Billy Boy?
    How old is she, charming Billy?
Twice one, twice two, twice eleven, but twenty-two,
    She's a young thing and cannot leave her mother.

9 February • Daisy Bell • Harry Dacre

Another comic love song, this time from the British music hall tradition, was written by Harry Dacre in 1892. Complaining to fellow songwriters that on arriving in America he was charged a customs fee for his bicycle, one friend replied – with a retort that gave Dacre the idea for the song – that it was lucky he didn't have a bicycle made for two. The chorus that begins, 'Daisy, Daisy, / Give me your answer, do!' has developed a life of its own as a nursery rhyme – even early computers were programmed to sing it in 1961, but you might find the recordings by the great Nat King Cole or Britpop's Blur more tuneful.

There is a flower within my heart, Daisy, Daisy!
Planted one day by a glancing dart,
Planted by Daisy Bell!
Whether she loves me or loves me not,
Sometimes it's hard to tell;
Yet I am longing to share the lot
Of beautiful Daisy Bell!

Daisy, Daisy,
Give me your answer, do!
I'm half crazy,
All for the love of you!
It won't be a stylish marriage,
I can't afford a carriage,
But you'll look sweet upon the seat
Of a bicycle built for two!

We will go 'tandem' as man and wife, Daisy, Daisy!
'Ped'ling' away down the road of life, I and my Daisy Bell!
When the road's dark we can both despise
P'liceman and 'lamps' as well;
There are 'bright lights' in the dazzling eyes
Of beautiful Daisy Bell!

Daisy, Daisy,
Give me your answer, do!
I'm half crazy,
All for the love of you!
It won't be a stylish marriage,
I can't afford a carriage,
But you'll look sweet upon the seat
Of a bicycle built for two!

I will stand by you in 'wheel' or woe, Daisy, Daisy!
You'll be the bell(e) which I'll ring you know!
Sweet little Daisy Bell!
You'll take the 'lead' in each 'trip' we take,
Then if I don't do well,
I will permit you to use the brake,
My beautiful Daisy Bell!

Daisy, Daisy,
Give me your answer, do!
I'm half crazy,
All for the love of you!
It won't be a stylish marriage,
I can't afford a carriage,
But you'll look sweet upon the seat
Of a bicycle built for two!

10 February • There was a Lady Loved a Swine • Anon.

This bizarre dialogue must have been popular throughout the seventeenth century, as it is referenced in two plays of that era. It's like something you'd hear in an episode of *Love Island*.

There was a lady loved a swine,
Honey, quoth she,
Pig-hog, wilt thou be mine?
'Hoogh,' quoth he.

I'll build thee a silver sty,
Honey, quoth she;
And in it thou shalt lie;
'Hoogh,' quoth he.

Pinned with a silver pin,
Honey, quoth she,
That thou mayst go out and in;
'Hoogh,' quoth he.

Wilt thou now have me,
Honey? quoth she;
'Hoogh, hoogh, hoogh!' quoth he,
And went his way.

11 February • A Cat Came Fiddling out of a Barn • Anon.

The previous entry had a lady loving a pig, but this is more like Edward Lear's 'The Owl and the Pussycat' (see 15 February), as it is a nonsense rhyme about an unlikely love between two different animals.

> A cat came fiddling out of a barn,
> With a pair of bag-pipes under her arm;
> She could sing nothing but, Fiddle cum fee,
> The mouse has married the humble-bee.
> Pipe, cat; dance, mouse;
> We'll have a wedding at our good house.

12 February • Cock Robin Got Up Early • Anon.

The wren is the UK's most common bird and the robin is the third most common, behind the chaffinch, who sadly gets no mention in this roundelay. (A 'roundelay' is a simple song with a refrain.)

Cock Robin got up early,
　　At the break of day,
And went to Jenny's window
　　To sing a roundelay.

He sang Cock Robin's love
　　To the little Jenny Wren,
And when he got unto the end,
　　Then he began again.

13 February • A Froggie Went a-Courtin' • Anon.

Unlikely as it might seem, recordings of this next interspecies romance have been made by some of American music's greatest legends, including Elvis Presley, Bob Dylan and Bruce Springsteen.

A Froggie went a-courtin' and he did ride;
Sword and pistol by his side.
He rode to Miss Mousie's hall,
Gave a loud knock and gave a loud call.

'Pray, Miss Mousie, are you within?'
'Yes, kind sir, I sit and spin.'
He took Miss Mousie on his knee,
And said, 'Miss Mousie, will you marry me?'

Miss Mousie blushed and hung her head,
'You'll have to ask Uncle Rat,' she said.
'Not without Uncle Rat's consent
Would I marry the President.'

Uncle Rat jumped up and shook his fat side,
To think his niece would be Bill Frog's bride.
Next day Uncle Rat went to town,
To buy his niece a nice wedding gown.

Where shall the wedding supper be?
Way down yonder in a hollow tree.
First to come in was a bumblebee,
Who played the fiddle on his knee.

The next to come was Captain Flea,
Danced a jig with the bumblebee.
Then Froggie and Mouse went off to France,
And that's the end of my romance.

14 February • Lavender's Blue, Dilly, Dilly • Anon.

Happy Valentine's Day! Familiarity with this seventeenth-century nursery rhyme was revived by its appearance in two Disney live-actions films: *So Dear to My Heart* in 1948, and *Cinderella* in 2015.

Lavender's blue, dilly, dilly,
  Lavender's green;
When I am king, dilly, dilly,
  You shall be queen.

Call up your men, dilly, dilly,
  Set them to work,
Some with a rake, dilly, dilly,
  Some with a fork.

Some to make hay, dilly, dilly,
  Some to thresh corn,
Whilst you and I, dilly, dilly,
  Keep ourselves warm.

15 February • The Owl and the Pussy-cat • Edward Lear

Depending on how your Valentine's Day went, you might be accustomed to finding nonsense not too far from love. Edward Lear (1812–1888) wrote this nonsense rhyme for a girl called Jane, the three-year-old daughter of his friends Catherine and John Addington Symonds.

The Owl and the Pussy-cat went to sea
  In a beautiful pea-green boat;
They took some honey, and plenty of money
  Wrapped up in a five-pound note.
The Owl looked up to the stars above,
  And sang to a small guitar,
'O lovely Pussy! O Pussy, my love,
  What a beautiful Pussy you are,
    You are,
    You are!
What a beautiful Pussy you are!'

Pussy said to the Owl, 'You elegant fowl!
  How charmingly sweet you sing!
O let us be married! Too long we have tarried:
  But what shall we do for a ring?'
They sailed away, for a year and a day,
  To the land where the Bong-tree grows
And there in a wood a Piggy-wig stood
  With a ring at the end of his nose,
    His nose,
    His nose,
With a ring at the end of his nose.

‘Dear Pig, are you willing to sell for one shilling
   Your ring?’ Said the Piggy, ‘I will.’
So they took it away, and were married next day
   By the Turkey who lives on the hill.
They dined on mince, and slices of quince,
   Which they ate with a runcible spoon;
And hand in hand, on the edge of the sand,
   They danced by the light of the moon,
         The moon,
         The moon,
They danced by the light of the moon.

16 February • Where Are You Going to, My Pretty Maid? • Anon.

In times of yore, certain districts in England recognized asking 'to go-a-milking' with a girl as tantamount to a marriage proposal – as in this rhyme, which tells of an unsuccessful proposal.

'Where are you going to, my pretty maid?'
'I'm going a-milking, sir,' she said.

'May I go with you, my pretty maid?'
'You're kindly welcome, sir,' she said.

'Say, will you marry me, my pretty maid?'
'Yes, if you please, kind sir,' she said.

'What is your father, my pretty maid?'
'My father's a farmer, sir,' she said.

'What is your fortune, my pretty maid?'
'My face is my fortune, sir,' she said.

'Then I can't marry you, my pretty maid.'
'Nobody asked you, sir,' she said.

17 February • Soldier, Soldier, Will You Marry Me? • Anon.

As the last rhyme shows, love and wooing do not always end well. This traditional song is accompanied by a two-player dressing-up game. One person is the soldier, and the other is the 'pretty girl' who has to try to run as fast as possible to get the hat, coat, boots and gloves to put on the soldier in time for the next verse.

Soldier, soldier, will you marry me,
With your musket, fife and drum?
Oh, how can I marry such a pretty girl as you,
When I have no hat to put on?

Off to the haberdasher she did go,
As fast as she could run,
Bought him a hat, the best that was there,
And the soldier put it on.

Soldier, soldier, will you marry me,
With your musket, fife and drum?
Oh, how can I marry such a pretty girl as you,
When I have no coat to put on?

Off to the tailor she did go,
As fast as she could run,
Bought him a coat, the best that was there,
And the soldier put it on.

Soldier, soldier, will you marry me,
With your musket, fife and drum?
Oh, how can I marry such a pretty girl as you,
When I have no boots to put on?

Off to the cobbler she did go,
As fast as she could run,
Bought him a pair of the best that was there,
And the soldier put them on.

Soldier, soldier, will you marry me,
With your musket, fife and drum?
Oh, how can I marry such a pretty girl as you,
When I have no gloves to put on?

Off to the glover she did go,
As fast as she could run,
Bought him a pair, the best that was there,
And the soldier put them on.

Soldier, soldier, will you marry me,
With your musket, fife and drum?
Oh, no, sweet maid, I cannot marry thee
For I have a wife at home.

18 February • Oh my Darling, Clementine • Anon.

This extract from the darkly comic nineteenth-century American folksong offers another example of ill-fated love (albeit more tragic than most) and the varied afterlives of nursery rhymes. The song's 'forty-niner' refers to the 1849 California Gold Rush; later, the first plutonium-fuelled fast-neutron reactor, built in 1946, was named Clementine after the song, as '49' was a code word for plutonium-239.

Oh my darling, oh my darling,
Oh my darling Clementine,
You are lost and gone forever,
Dreadful sorry, Clementine.

In a cavern, in a canyon,
Excavating for a mine,
Dwelt a miner, forty-niner,
And his daughter, Clementine.

Oh my darling, oh my darling,
Oh my darling, Clementine
You are lost and gone forever
Dreadful sorry, Clementine.

Light she was and like a fairy
And her shoes were number nine,
Herring boxes, without topses,
Sandals were for Clementine.

Oh my darling, oh my darling,
Oh my darling Clementine,
You are lost and gone forever,
Dreadful sorry, Clementine.

19 February • My Baby has a Mottled Fist • Christina Rossetti

Now we move on to family love. The Victorian poet Christina Rossetti (1830–1894) wrote this for *Sing-Song*, her collection of poems for the nursery.

My baby has a mottled fist,
    My baby has a neck in creases;
My baby kisses and is kissed,
    For he's the very thing for kisses.

20 February • I Love You Well, my Little Brother • Anon.

Perhaps some of the strongest family relationships are those between siblings, the subject of these next four rhymes.

I love you well, my little brother,
    And you are fond of me;
Let us be kind to one another,
    As brothers ought to be.
You shall learn to play with me,
    And learn to use my toys;
And then I think that we shall be
    Two happy little boys.

21 February • My Sister • Giles Andreae

Today's rhyme about sibling love is by the best-selling poet Giles Andreae, who grew up with three brothers and no sister.

I never had a sister.
She never did exist.
So I never could have kissed her,
And that's one thing I've missed.

22 February • Molly, My Sister, and I Fell Out • Anon.

Not all siblings get on well, and their arguments can be about the slightest of differences . . .

Molly, my sister, and I fell out,
And what do you think it was all about?
She loved coffee and I loved tea,
And that was the reason we couldn't agree.

23 February • Fudge, Fudge, Call the Judge! • Anon.

In this American rope-skipping rhyme, the speaker is clearly not thrilled about the arrival of a sibling. The harsh treatment of the infant follows a tradition of playfully dark scenarios across nursery rhymes and fairy tales alike.

Fudge, fudge,
Call the judge.
Mama's got a baby.
Ain't no girl,
Ain't no boy,
Just a plain old baby.
Wrap it up in tissue paper.
Put it on the elevator.
First floor, miss!
Second floor, miss!
Third floor, miss!
Fourth floor –
Pop it out the door.

24 February • My Grandfather's Clock • Henry Clay Work

This lovely one about a grandfather was written by the American songwriter Henry Clay Work (1832–1884), and is credited with coining the term 'grandfather clock'. The great singers Johnny Cash, Bing Crosby and Sam Cooke have all made it their own.

My grandfather's clock was too large for the shelf,
So it stood ninety years on the floor;
It was taller by half than the old man himself,
Though it weighed not a pennyweight more.
It was bought on the morn of the day that he was born,
And was always his treasure and pride;
But it stopped short – never to go again –
When the old man died.

Ninety years without slumbering
(Tick, tick, tick, tick),
His life seconds numbering,
(Tick, tick, tick, tick),
It stopped short – never to go again –
When the old man died.

In watching its pendulum swing to and fro,
Many hours had he spent while a boy.
And in childhood and manhood the clock seemed to know
And to share both his grief and his joy.
For it struck twenty-four when he entered at the door,
With a blooming and beautiful bride;
But it stopped short – never to go again –
When the old man died.

Ninety years without slumbering
(Tick, tick, tick, tick),
His life seconds numbering,
(Tick, tick, tick, tick),
It stopped short – never to go again –
When the old man died.

My grandfather said that of those he could hire,
Not a servant so faithful he found;
For it wasted no time, and had but one desire –
At the close of each week to be wound.
And it kept in its place – not a frown upon its face,
And its hands never hung by its side.
But it stopp'd short – never to go again –
When the old man died.

Ninety years without slumbering
(Tick, tick, tick, tick),
His life seconds numbering,
(Tick, tick, tick, tick),
It stopped short – never to go again –
When the old man died.

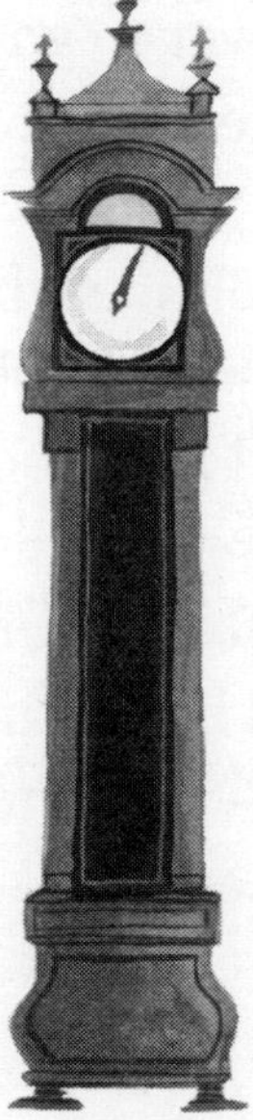

It rang an alarm in the dead of the night –
An alarm that for years had been dumb;
And we knew that his spirit was pluming for flight –
That his hour of departure had come.
Still the clock kept the time, with a soft and muffled chime,
As we silently stood by his side;
But it stopped short – never to go again –
When the old man died.

Ninety years without slumbering
(Tick, tick, tick, tick),
His life seconds numbering,
(Tick, tick, tick, tick),
It stopped short – never to go again –
When the old man died.

25 February • The More We Get Together • Anon.

The love between friends can be just as important as that between family and lovers. The following was a popular hit in the American TV Show *Barney & Friends*, sung by Barney, the purple dinosaur.

The more we get together, together, together
The more we get together, the happier we'll be!
'Cos your friends are my friends and my friends are your
  friends,
The more we get together, the happier we'll be!

26 February • Collop Monday • Anon.

Now we come to Shrovetide, the week-long tradition with which Pancake Day and Lent are associated. Collop Monday is the first day, so named after the tradition of feasting on 'collops' (small pieces of meat, especially bacon); Pancake Tuesday (also known as Mardi Gras, meaning 'Fat Tuesday') was an opportunity to use up any remaining milk, flour and eggs; Ash Wednesday is the beginning of the fast, so called because worshippers have their foreheads marked with crosses of ash. The 'Bludee Thursday' and 'Friday lang' might just be named for this rhyme, although there is an English tradition from the twelfth century, which still occurs in a few places, where villagers assemble to play a yearly Shrovetime game with a football that would often get quite bloody! This ended in most regions with the 1875 Highways Act, banning football in public spaces.

Collop Monday,
Pancake Tuesday,
Ash Wednesday,
Bludee Thursday,
Friday's lang, but will be dune,
And hey for Saturday afternune!

27 February • Mix a Pancake • Christina Rossetti

This Pancake Day rhyme is another marvel by Christina Rossetti.

Mix a pancake,
Stir a pancake,
    Pop it in the pan;
Fry the pancake,
Toss the pancake –
    Catch it if you can.

28 February • Dibbity, Dibbity, Doe • Anon.

Here is a final, nonsensical rhyme for Shrovetide that has been around since 1842.

Dibbity, dibbity, doe,
Give me a pancake and I'll go.

Dibbity, dibbity, dibbity, ditter,
Please to give me a bit of a fritter.

29 February • Thirty Days Hath September • Anon.

Remembering the number of days in each month is a struggle the world over. In China, for instance, children are taught to remember which months are longer by counting them along their knuckles. This rhyme is one of the oldest in the book; a French variant can be traced back to the 1200s and a favourite anonymous response goes like this: 'Thirty days hath September / All the rest I can't remember . . .'

Thirty days hath September,
April, June, and November.
All the rest have thirty-one,
Except February alone,
Which has four and twenty-four
Till leap-year gives it one day more.

March

Spring, Women's Day, Riddles

1 March • On the First of March • Anon.

With March comes the beginning of spring, and the steady return of flora and fauna. Many nursery rhymes work as a meteorological apparatus helping us to predict changes in weather, carrying a tradition known as weather lore. Examples can be found in these next three entries.

On the first of March,
The crows begin to search;
By the first of April,
They are sitting still;
By the first of May,
They're all flown away;
Crowping greedy back again,
With October's wind and rain.

2 March • Crow on the Fence • Anon.

We are out of the practice of heeding the wisdom of weather lore, but the behaviour of birds has been used to predict the weather throughout history, due to their remarkable ability to react to changes in air pressure.

Crow on the fence,
Rain will go hence.
Crow on the ground,
Rain will come down.

3 March • March Winds, April Showers • Anon.

This weather lore puts a positive spin on the spring weather.

March winds, April showers
Bring forth May flowers.

4 March • When I Was a Little Girl • Anon.

As we lead up to International Women's Day on 8 March, it is a fitting time to include this run of rhymes. The first is set in Darlington, a town in County Durham, in the North of England. A 'kirk' is a Northern English and Scottish word for 'church'.

When I was a little girl,
  About seven years old,
I hadn't got a petticoat,
  To keep me from the cold.

So I went into Darlington,
  That pretty little town,
And there I bought a petticoat,
  A cloak, and a gown.

I went into the woods
  And built me a kirk,
And all the birds of the air,
  They helped me to work.

The hawk, with his long claws,
  Pulled down the stone,
The dove, with her rough bill,
  Brought me them home.

The parrot was the clergyman,
  The peacock was the clerk,
The bullfinch played the organ,
  And we made merry work.

5 March • What Are Little Boys Made of? • Robert Southey

The Poet Laureate Robert Southey (1774–1843) is said to have penned this popular nursery rhyme. Beyond the huge amount of poetry he wrote (his collected poems fill ten volumes!), Southey is also notable for having written the original story of 'Goldilocks and the Three Bears'.

What are little boys made of?
What are little boys made of?
    Frogs and snails
    And puppy-dogs' tails,
That's what little boys are made of.

What are little girls made of?
What are little girls made of?
    Sugar and spice
    And all that's nice,
That's what little girls are made of.

6 March • There Was an Old Woman Called Nothing-at-all • Anon.

First printed in 1641, this rhyme was particularly popular in the reign of Charles I (1625–49).

> There was an old woman called Nothing-at-all,
> Who rejoiced in a dwelling exceedingly small;
> A man stretched his mouth to its utmost extent,
> And down at one gulp house and old woman went.

7 March • There Was a Little Girl • Henry Wadsworth Longfellow

This children's poem – much recited across the English speaking world – is attributed to the American poet Henry Wadsworth Longfellow (1807–1882). Although Longfellow did say, 'When I recall my juvenile poems [. . .] I wish sometimes that they were forgotten entirely.' This poem is as well-known today as any of his acclaimed narrative work, such as *The Song of Hiawatha*, so even if he didn't write it, let's hope he'd forgive us for including it here.

> There was a little girl, and she had a little curl
> Right in the middle of her forehead;
> When she was good, she was very, very good,
> But when she was bad, she was horrid.

8 March • There Was a Little Girl • Anon.

Happy International Women's Day! This reworking of the previous rhyme was written in a 1912 pamphlet in support of the Suffragettes.

There was a little girl and she had a little curl
Right down the middle of her forehead.
When she got the vote she was very good, indeed,
But when they kept it from her she was horrid.

9 March • This Little Pig Went to Business • Anon.

Here is another verse from the same Suffragette pamphlet, this time a rewrite of the well-known rhyme 'This Little Pig went to Market' (see 21 May).

This little pig went to business;
This little pig stayed home;
This little pig had the suffrage;
This little pig had none;
This little pig said, 'Wee, wee, wee,
I'm going to get it some day!'

10 March • There Was an Old Woman Tossed up in a Basket • Anon.

This nursery rhyme was first printed in the early eighteenth century. It was a favourite of the Anglo-Irish playwright Oliver Goldsmith (1728–1774), who is said to have sung this rhyme to himself in the early hours of 29 January 1768, in an attempt to cheer himself up after his comedy *The Good-Natur'd Man* was poorly received on its opening night.

There was an old woman tossed up in a basket,
Seventeen times as high as the moon;
Where she was going I couldn't but ask it,
For in her hand she carried a broom.
Old woman, old woman, old woman, quoth I,
Where are you going to up so high?
To brush the cobwebs off the sky!
May I go with you?
Aye, by-and-by.

11 March • There Was an Old Woman who Lived in a Shoe • Anon.

This eighteenth-century rhyme recalls the perhaps surprising association of shoes with female fertility. The tradition of tying a shoe to the bumper of a newly married couple's car is a relic of this.

There was an old woman who lived in a shoe,
She had so many children she didn't know what to do;
She gave them some broth without any bread;
She whipped them all soundly and put them to bed.

12 March • You Know the Old Woman who Lived in a Shoe? • Beatrix Potter

Beatrix Potter (1866–1943), the much-loved author of the Peter Rabbit series, published illustrated books of nursery rhymes later in her career. This is her charming reimagining of the previous rhyme.

You know the old woman who lived in a shoe,
And had so many children she didn't know what to do?
I think if she lived in a little shoe-house –
That little old woman was surely a mouse!

13 March • There Was an Old Woman of Leeds • R. S. Sharpe

This limerick appears in the first ever book of limericks, *The History of Sixteen Wonderful Old Women* (1821). It was likely written by R. S. Sharpe, who might be the only writer ever described as 'a grocer who dabbled in poetry'.

There was an old woman of Leeds,
Who spent all her time in good deeds;
    She worked for the poor
    Till her fingers were sore,
This pious old woman of Leeds.

14 March • In Spring I Look Gay • Anon.

Now we welcome a run of riddles. As spring's blooms unfurl, this first one is seasonal. As a hint, 'comely array' refers to attractive garments.

In Spring I look gay,
Decked in comely array,
In Summer more clothing I wear;
When colder it grows,
I fling off my clothes,
And in Winter quite naked appear.

[Answer: a tree]

15 March • There's a Wee, Wee House • Anon.

You might guess this next one. There's a clue to be found in 'Humpty Dumpty' (see 2 November).

There's a wee, wee house,
And it's full of meat;
But neither door nor window
Will let you in to eat.

[Answer: an egg]

16 March • Elizabeth, Elspeth, Betsy and Bess • Anon.

This is a slightly more complicated riddle, which asks you to work out how its seemingly impossible statements could make sense. You wouldn't want to find this one in a maths exam.

Elizabeth, Elspeth, Betsy and Bess,
They all went together to seek a bird's nest.
They found a bird's nest with five eggs in,
They all took one, and left four in.

[Answer: Elizabeth, Elspeth, Betsy and Bess
are all versions of the same name]

17 March • Two Legs Sat Upon Three Legs • Anon.

These next few riddles try *very* hard to confound you.

Two legs sat upon three legs,
With one leg in his lap;
In comes four legs,
Runs away with one leg,
Up jumps two legs,
Catches up three legs,
Throws it after four legs,
And makes him bring back one leg.

[Answer: Four legs belong to a dog, three to a stool,
two to a human, and one to a leg of mutton]

18 March • Two Brothers We Are • Anon.

A clue that refers back to 11 March: these brothers might find themselves a bit busy after a wedding!

Two brothers we are, great burdens we bear,
    On which we are bitterly pressed;
The truth is to say, we are full all the day,
    And empty when we go to rest.

[Answer: The two brothers are shoes]

19 March • As I Was Going o'er Westminster Bridge • Anon.

Perhaps the most famous poem ever written about Westminster Bridge is by William Wordsworth (1770–1850), but William isn't the hidden answer here.

As I was going o'er Westminster Bridge,
    I met with a Westminster scholar;
He pulled off his cap, *an' drew* off his glove,
    And wished me a very good morrow.
What is his name?

[Answer: Andrew]

20 March • As I Went Through a Field of Wheat • Anon.

The answer to this one is a strangely popular choice for riddles.

> As I went through a field of wheat,
> I picked up something good to eat;
> It had neither flesh nor bone,
> But in twenty-one days it walked alone.

[Answer: An egg]

21 March • Purple, Yellow, Red and Green • Anon.

Here's an English Civil War-era riddle whose date can be estimated thanks to its reference to 'old Noll'. This was a nickname given to the leading Parliamentarian Oliver Cromwell (1599–1658) by his Royalist opponents.

> Purple, yellow, red and green,
> The King cannot reach it, nor the Queen;
> Nor can old Noll, whose power's so great:
> Tell me this riddle while I count eight.

[Answer: A rainbow]

22 March • Runs All Day and Never Walks • Anon.

As a hint, this riddle uses the word 'murmur' in its broadest sense: an 'irregular flow'.

Runs all day and never walks,
Often murmurs, never talks.
It has a bed, but never sleeps,
It has a mouth, but never eats.

[Answer: A river]

23 March • As I Was Going to St Ives • Anon.

Be warned: this tongue-twisting riddle contains a trap . . .

As I was going to St Ives,
I met a man with seven wives;
Each wife had seven sacks,
Each sack had seven cats,
Each cat had seven kits:
Kits, cats, sacks, and wives,
How many were going to St Ives?

[Answer: one. It is designed to convince you to multiply by the number 7, which would give you the answer 2,401 – but only the speaker is going to St Ives]

24 March • Higgledy-Piggledy • Anon.

This tricky rhyme is a literary 'charade' – an old-fashioned word-guessing game similar to a cryptic crossword. Each syllable of the answer is enigmatically described as its own word 'first' and 'second', and the entire word is described by the 'Higgledy-piggledy' refrain.

Higgledy-piggledy
Here we lie,
Picked and plucked,
And put in a pie.
My first is snapping, snarling, growling,
My second's hard-working, romping, and prowling.
Higgledy-piggledy
Here we lie,
Picked and plucked
And put in a pie.

[Answer: The first syllable is *cur* (an old word
to describe dogs), and the second is *ants*, so
the answer is . . . currants!]

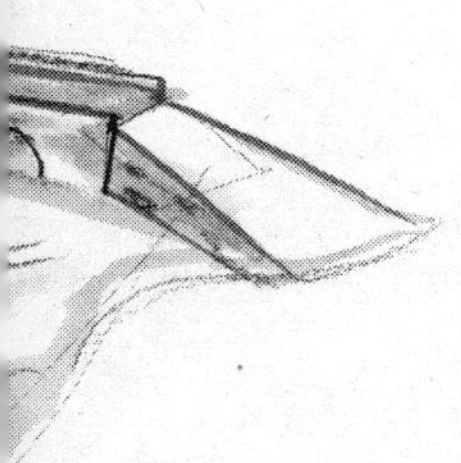

25 March • For Want of a Nail • Anon.

Today's entry refers to the Battle of Bosworth and echoes Richard III's memorably expressed plea in Shakespeare's history play, 'A horse, a horse, my kingdom for a horse!' While riddles try to trick you, this is is a proverb that sets out to offer some wisdom.

For want of a nail, the shoe was lost,
For want of the shoe, the horse was lost,
For want of a horse, the rider was lost,
For want of a rider, the battle was lost,
For want of the battle, the kingdom was lost,
And all for the want of a horseshoe nail.

26 March • When a Great Tree Falls • Anon.

Some riddles don't have a clear answer, such as this one.

When a great tree falls
And people aren't near,
Does it make a noise
If no one can hear?
And which came first,
The hen or the egg?
This impractical question
We ask and then beg.
Some wise men say
It's beyond their ken.
Did anyone ever
Ask the hen?

27 March • I Saw a Peacock with a Fiery Tail • Anon.

The next confusing rhyme might have been composed to teach the importance of using commas.

I saw a peacock with a fiery tail
I saw a blazing comet drop down hail
I saw a cloud with ivy curled around
I saw a sturdy oak creep on the ground
I saw an ant swallow up a whale
I saw a raging sea brim full of ale
I saw a Venice glass sixteen foot deep
I saw a well full of men's tears that weep
I saw their eyes all in a flame of fire
I saw a house high as the moon and higher
I saw the sun at twelve o'clock at night
I saw the man who saw this wondrous sight.

28 March • Who Killed Cock Robin? • Anon.

This might be one of the oldest entries we have – so old that 'owl' is made to rhyme with 'shovel', which, back in the fourteenth century, was pronounced 'showell'. Incidentally, Alfred Hitchcock's movie *Sabotage* featured the 1935 Silly Symphonies cartoon version of 'Who Killed Cock Robin?' and a few decades later, the American folk singer (and Nobel Prize winner) Bob Dylan used the rhyme's structure for his 1963 song about the death of a boxer in the ring, 'Who Killed Davey Moore'.

Who killed Cock Robin?
  I, said the Sparrow,
  With my bow and arrow,
I killed Cock Robin.

Who saw him die?
  I, said the Fly,
  With my little eye,
I saw him die.

Who caught his blood?
  I, said the Duck,
  It was just my luck,
I caught his blood.

Who'll make the shroud?
  I, said the Beetle,
  With my thread and needle,
I'll make the shroud.

Who'll dig his grave?
  I, said the Owl,
  With my pick and shovel,
I'll dig his grave.

Who'll be the parson?
  I, said the Rook,
  With my little book,
I'll be the parson.

Who'll be the clerk?
  I, said the Lark,
  If it's not in the dark,
I'll be the clerk.

Who'll carry the link?
  I, said the Linnet,
  I'll fetch it in a minute,
I'll carry the link.

Who'll be chief mourner?
  I, said the Dove,
  I mourn for my love,
I'll be chief mourner.

Who'll carry the coffin?
  I, said the Kite,
  If it's not through the night,
I'll carry the coffin.

Who'll bear the pall?
  I, said the Crow,
  With the cock and the bow,
I'll bear the pall.

Who'll sing a psalm?
  I, said the Thrush,
  As she sat on a bush,
I'll sing a psalm.

Who'll toll the bell?
  I, said the Bull,
  Because I can pull,
I'll toll the bell.

  All the birds of the air
  Fell a-sighing and a-sobbing
  When they heard the bell toll
  For poor Cock Robin.

NOTICE:
  To all it concerns,
  This notice apprises,
  The Sparrow's for trial
  At next bird assizes.

29 March • Which is the Bow that Has No Arrow? • Anon.

This seasonal question-rhyme follows a call-and-response pattern, where the riddle is answered in the following line.

> Which is the bow that has no arrow?
> (The rainbow, that never killed a sparrow.)
> Which is the singer that has but one song?
> (The cuckoo, who singeth it all day long.)

30 March • What is Pink? • Christina Rossetti

The wondrous colours found in nature are celebrated in this poem from the collection *Sing-Song* (1893) by the Victorian poet Christina Rossetti.

> What is pink? A rose is pink
> By the fountain's brink.
> What is red? A poppy's red
> In its barley bed.
> What is blue? The sky is blue
> Where the clouds float through.
> What is white? A swan is white
> Sailing in the light.

What is yellow? Pears are yellow,
Rich and ripe and mellow.
What is green? The grass is green,
With small flowers between.
What is violet? Clouds are violet
In the summer twilight.
What is orange? Why, an orange,
Just an orange!

31 March • I Had a Nickel and I Walked Around the Block • Anon.

For the last day of the month, here is an American rhyme to get us in the mood for April Fool's Day. A 'nickel' is a five-cent US coin.

I had a nickel and I walked around the block;
I walked right into a baker shop.
I took two doughnuts right out of the grease;
I handed the lady my five-cent piece.
She looked at the nickel and she looked at me,
And said, 'This money's no good to me.
There's a hole in the nickel, and it goes right through.'
Says I, 'There's a hole in the doughnut, too.'

April

April Fool's Day, Spring Festivals, Tongue Twisters

1 April • Anna Elise, She Jumped with Surprise • Anon.

Happy April Fool's Day! The traditional couplet to recite after you've tricked someone is 'Fool, fool, April fool, / You learn nought by going to school!' You should remember, however, that the period for fooling only extends to noon, and if anyone springs their high jinks on you after that hour, you should respond with 'April Fool time's past and gone, / You're the fool, and I'm none!' To celebrate the day, here is a rhyme that is thought to have been around since the fourteenth century.

Anna Elise, she jumped with surprise;
The surprise was so quick, it played her a trick;
The trick was so rare, she jumped in a chair;
The chair was so frail, she jumped in a pail;
The pail was so wet, she jumped in a net;
The net was so small, she jumped on the ball;
The ball was so round, she jumped on the ground;
And ever since then she's been turning around.

2 April • One Bright Morning in the Middle of the Night • Anon.

A run of nonsense verse begins with this rhyme of contradictory and impossible happenings, There are multiple mutations of this poem, with an early piece from 1380 (found in the Bodleian Library) beginning, 'I saw three headless [men] playing at a ball, / A handless man served them all./

While three mouthless men laughed, / Three legless [men] from them ran.'

> One bright morning in the middle of the night,
> Two dead boys got up to fight.
> They turned their backs and faced each other,
> Drew their swords and shot the other.
> One was blind and the other couldn't see,
> So they chose a fool for their referee.
> A deaf policeman heard the noise.
> He came and shot the two dead boys.
> A legless donkey passing by,
> Kicked the copper in the eye,
> And knocked him through a rubber wall,
> Into a dry ditch and drowned them all.
> If you don't believe this lie is true,
> Ask the blind man. He saw it too.

3 April • The Man in the Wilderness Said to Me • Anon.

The Victorian folklorist and theatre historian James Orchard Halliwell-Phillipps (1820–1889) collected this nonsense rhyme from a manuscript from the 1600s.

> The man in the wilderness said to me,
> 'How many strawberries grow in the sea?'
> I answered him, as I thought good,
> 'As many red herrings as grow in the wood.'

4 April • On the Ning Nang Nong • Spike Milligan

Anybody considering a quiet Easter getaway might want to avoid the place that's the subject of this nonsense rhyme – full of nonsense words – by the poet Spike Milligan (1918–2002). Though you may not want to visit, this was once voted the UK's favourite comic poem.

On the Ning Nang Nong
Where the Cows go Bong!
And the monkeys all say BOO!
There's a Nong Nang Ning
Where the trees go Ping!
And the teapots jibber jabber joo.
On the Nong Ning Nang
All the mice go Clang
And you just can't catch 'em when they do!
So it's Ning Nang Nong
The cows go Bong!
Nong Nang Ning
The trees go Ping!
Nong Ning Nang
The mice go Clang!
What a noisy place to belong
Is the Ning Nang Ning Nang Nong!!

5 April • There Was an Old Man with a Beard • Edward Lear

The king of limericks would have to be the Victorian poet Edward Lear (1812–1888), who popularized the form. His work was a big influence on Spike Milligan (see opposite).

There was an Old Man with a beard,
Who said, 'It is just as I feared!—
  Two Owls and a Hen,
  Four Larks and a Wren,
Have all built their nests in my beard!'

6 April • A Diner While Dining at Crewe • Anon.

Like Lear's limerick above, this anonymous example again waits until the last line to deliver its surprise.

A diner while dining at Crewe
Found quite a large mouse in his stew.
  Said the waiter, 'Don't shout,
  And wave it about,
Or the rest will be wanting one, too.'

7 April • A Man with an Enormous Nose • Michael Rosen

Contemporary poets have also had fun with the limerick form. We have children's poet Michael Rosen to thank for this unforgettable image.

A man with an enormous nose
Used to put on fantastic shows.
    In his nose he'd squeeze
    A swarm of bees,
A cabbage and most of his toes.

8 April • A Rub • John Bannister Tabb

The following runny-nosed rhyme is by the American poet John Bannister Tabb (1845–1909). Its title – 'A Rub' – jokes about an old meaning of 'rub', as an obstacle or point of difference ('To sleep, perchance to dream – ay, there's the rub,' as Shakespeare's Hamlet says).

> 'Twixt Handkerchief and Nose
> A difference arose;
> And a tradition goes
> That they settled it by blows.

9 April • John Brown's Baby • Anon.

This song is sung to the tune of the Battle Hymn of the Republic, and requires at least some coordination on the singer's part. Some very simple actions accompany the tune: a salute at the mention of 'John Brown', a rocking baby motion for 'baby', a cough for 'cold', a pat on the chest for 'chest', a chest-rubbing motion for 'rubbed', and holding your nose for 'camphorated oil'. To make it more complicated, remove one of these words each time you sing the verse, and instead of the word, make the action!

> John Brown's baby had a cold upon his chest,
> John Brown's baby had a cold upon his chest,
> John Brown's baby had a cold upon his chest,
> And they rubbed it with camphorated oil.

10 April • Tweedledum and Tweedledee • Anon.

Another parody, echoing an eighteenth-century verse by John Byrom about a rivalry between two composers (Handel and Bononcini), was silly enough to make its way into Wonderland. It features in Lewis Carroll's second Alice book, *Through the Looking-Glass* (1871), when Alice meets Dum and Dee and is reminded of the nursery rhyme.

Tweedledum and Tweedledee
  Resolved to have a battle;
For Tweedledum said Tweedledee
  Had spoiled his nice new rattle.

Just then flew by a monstrous crow,
  As big as a tar-barrel;
Which frightened both the heroes so,
  They quite forgot their quarrel.

11 April • Hot Cross Buns! • Anon.

April is a month for religious holidays, beginning with this one for the Christian festival of Easter. This nursery rhyme was originally a market trader's street-cry, but over time it became a folk chant for Good Friday, when hot cross buns are customarily enjoyed. Since then, it has also turned into a children's game similar to One Potato (see 11 September). Avoid this poem on an empty stomach.

Hot cross buns!
Hot cross buns!
One a penny, two a penny,
Hot cross buns!
If you have no daughters,
Give them to your sons;
One a penny, two a penny,
Hot cross buns!

12 April • Ramadan! Hamadan! Here I Come! • Uzo Unobagha

The month of Ramadan inspired a modern nursery rhyme written by Nigerian author Uzo Unobagha. Ramadan is the ninth month of the Islamic calendar, lasting from one crescent moon until the next, and commemorates the Prophet Muhammad (PBUH)'s first revelation. Muslims worldwide celebrate it as a month for reflection, community, praying and fasting – hence the 'hungry chum'. This poem is more appropriate for an empty stomach than yesterday's!

Ramadan! Hamadan! Here I come!
With my spoon, and cup, and plate,
With Abdul, my hungry chum,
Ramadan! Hamadan! Don't be late!

13 April • Chad Gadya • Anon.

Also known as Pesach, Passover is a Jewish holiday celebrating the exodus of Israelites from slavery in Egypt. It falls between the fifteenth and twenty-second days of the Hebrew month of Nisan, which is normally during April. This traditional nursery rhyme is in the Haggadah (a text compiled some time between the second and fourth century), which is read each Passover, making it one of the first verses written specifically for children. It takes the form of a cumulative rhyme, and was known to inspire 'This is the House that Jack Built' (see 24 July).

One little goat, one little goat
That father bought for two zuzim.
One little goat, one little goat.

Then came a cat
And ate the goat,
That father bought for two zuzim.
One little goat, one little goat.

Then came a dog
And bit the cat,
That ate the goat,
That father bought for two zuzim.
One little goat, one little goat.

Then came a stick
And beat the dog,
That bit the cat,
That ate the goat,
That father bought for two zuzim.
One little goat, one little goat.

Then came a fire
And burnt the stick,
That beat the dog,
That bit the cat,
That ate the goat,
That father bought for two zuzim.
One little goat, one little goat.

Then came water
And quenched the fire,
That burnt the stick,
That beat the dog,
That bit the cat,
That ate the goat,
That father bought for two zuzim.
One little goat, one little goat.

Then came an ox
And drank the water,
That quenched the fire,
That burnt the stick,
That beat the dog,
That bit the cat,
That ate the goat,
That father bought for two zuzim.
One little goat, one little goat.

Then came the slaughterer
And slaughtered the ox,
That drank the water,
That quenched the fire,
That burnt the stick,

That beat the dog,
That bit the cat,
That ate the goat,
That father bought for two zuzim.
One little goat, one little goat.

Then came the Angel of Death,
And killed the slaughterer,
That slaughtered the ox,
That drank the water,
That quenched the fire,
That burnt the stick,
That beat the dog,
That bit the cat,
That ate the goat,
That father bought for two zuzim.
One little goat, one little goat.

Then came the Holy One, Blessed be He
And smote the Angel of Death,
That killed the slaughterer,
That slaughtered the ox,
That drank the water,
That quenched the fire,
That burnt the stick,
That beat the dog,
That bit the cat,
That ate the goat,
That father bought for two zuzim.
One little goat, one little goat.

14 April • We Are the Khalsa • Anon.

Vaisakhi is a Sikh festival celebrating the founding of the Khalsa in 1699 by Guru Gobind Singh (1666–1708). Khalsa is a Sikh warrior community, created to fight against cruelty. This is a modern nursery rhyme for Vaisakhi, using a call-and-response structure.

> We are the Khalsa (We are the Khalsa)
> Mighty, mighty Khalsa (Mighty, mighty Khalsa)
> Everywhere we go (Everywhere we go)
> People want to know (People want to know)
> Who we are (Who we are)
> So we tell them (So we tell them)
> We are the children of (We are the children of)
> Guru Gobind Singh Ji!

15 April · In April Come He Will · Anon.

There is an old saying in England: 'the cuckoo sings from St Tiburtius' Day to St John's Day' (14 April until 24 June). Appropriately enough, the Saturday closest to 14 April is known as Cuckoo Day, celebrating the return of the common cuckoo, and generally welcoming the advancing spring.

In April come he will.
In May he sings all day.
In June he changes tune,
In July he flies away.

16 April • The Cuckoo's a Bonnie Bird • Anon.

Our second cuckoo rhyme is the Scots variant of an English folk song, and is another example of a nursery rhyme to be found in music's hall of fame. Bob Dylan's album *Live at the Gaslight* (1962) contains an adaptation of it: 'The cuckoo is a pretty bird / And she warbles as she flies.'

The cuckoo's a bonnie bird,
He sings as he flies;
He brings us good tidings,
He tells us nae lies.

He drinks the cold water,
To keep his voice clear;
And he'll come again
In the spring of the year.

17 April • Hop, Little Bunnies • Anon.

As April moves along, we turn our focus from cuckoos to other springtime animals, with this sweet action song. Children act out the role of the sleeping bunnies, then wake up to 'hop, hop, hop' – often with great excitement.

See the little bunnies sleeping
Till it's nearly noon
Shall we wake them
With a merry tune?
They're so still, are they ill?
Wake up soon.
Wake up, bunnies!
Hop, little bunnies, hop, hop, hop,
Hop, little bunnies, hop, hop, hop,
Hop, little bunnies, hop, hop, hop,
Hop and stop.

18 April • Mary Had a Little Lamb • Sarah Josepha Hale

The teacher and poet Sarah Josepha Hale (1788–1879) gave us this much-loved nursery rhyme, apparently inspired by a real event. The famous opening stanza was the first ever recording made on American inventor Thomas Edison's new phonograph machine in 1877.

Mary had a little lamb,
With fleece as white as snow;
And everywhere that Mary went,
The lamb was sure to go.

It followed her to school one day,
Which was against the rule;
And made the children laugh and play,
To see a lamb at school.

And so the teacher turned it out,
But still it lingered near,
And waited patiently about,
Till Mary did appear.

'What makes the lamb love Mary so?'
The eager children cry,
'Why, Mary loves the lamb, you know!'
The teacher did reply.

19 April • Little Bo-Peep Has Lost Her Sheep • Anon.

A much less diligent shepherdess than Mary, Little Bo-Peep is associated with the game of hide-and-seek, which is known as bo-peep in parts of South West England. While it is unclear whether the rhyme existed in Jacobean England, the hiding game of bo-peep must have done, as it is referenced in Shakespeare's *King Lear* (Act 1, Scene 4): 'That such a king should play bo-peep.'

Little Bo-Peep has lost her sheep,
And can't tell where to find them;
Leave them alone, and they'll come home,
Bringing their tails behind them.

Little Bo-Peep fell fast asleep,
And dreamt she heard them bleating;
But when she awoke, she found it a joke,
For they were still all fleeting.

Then up she took her little crook,
Determined for to find them;
She found them indeed, but it made
her heart bleed,
For they'd left their tails behind them.

It happened one day, as Bo-Peep did stray
Into a meadow hard by,
There she espied their tails, side by side,
All hung on a tree to dry.

She heaved a sigh, and wiped her eye,
And over the hillocks she raced;
And tried what she could, as a
shepherdess should,
That each tail be properly placed.

20 April • Baa, Baa, Black Sheep • Anon.

The last thing you might expect to emerge from changes in export law would be an enduring nursery rhyme. And yet, the introduction of an export tax on wool in 1275 appears to have inspired this childhood favourite – but it also has a simpler and often overlooked meaning. Black sheep are not as profitable for farmers, as their wool can't be dyed; for some farmers in rural Scotland they are a symbol of bad luck. The phrase 'black sheep' has come to refer to an unwanted outsider.

Baa, baa, black sheep,
    Have you any wool?
Yes, sir, yes, sir,
    Three bags full;
One for the master,
    And one for the dame,
And one for the little boy
    Who lives down the lane.

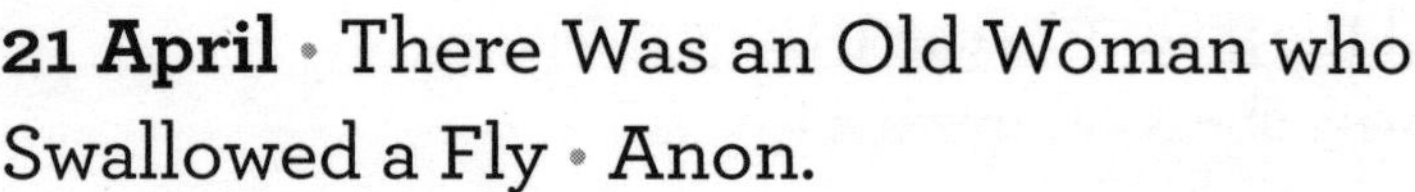

21 April • There Was an Old Woman who Swallowed a Fly • Anon.

The cumulative structure (see 13 April) of this next rhyme about a woman with questionable problem-solving capabilities is taken to the level of the absurd. The nonsensical story first appeared in print around the mid-twentieth century. The folk singer Judy Collins performed it alongside a shadow puppet in a 1977 episode of *The Muppet Show*, and it has been adapted into a feminist poem that begins: 'There was a young woman who swallowed a lie'.

There was an old woman who swallowed a fly,
I don't know why she swallowed a fly,
Perhaps she'll die!

There was an old woman who swallowed a spider,
That wriggled and jiggled and tickled inside her.
She swallowed the spider to catch the fly,
I don't know why she swallowed a fly,
Perhaps she'll die!

There was an old woman who swallowed a bird,
How absurd to swallow a bird.
She swallowed the bird to catch the spider
That wriggled and jiggled and tickled inside her.
She swallowed the spider to catch the fly,
I don't know why she swallowed a fly,
Perhaps she'll die!

There was an old woman who swallowed a cat,
Fancy that! She swallowed a cat!
She swallowed the cat to catch the bird,
She swallowed the bird to catch the spider
That wriggled and jiggled and tickled inside her.

She swallowed the spider to catch the fly,
I don't know why she swallowed a fly,
Perhaps she'll die!

There was an old woman that swallowed a dog,
She went the whole hog, and swallowed a dog!
She swallowed the dog to catch the cat,
She swallowed the cat to catch the bird,
She swallowed the bird to catch the spider
That wriggled and jiggled and tickled inside her.
She swallowed the spider to catch the fly,
Perhaps she'll die!

There was an old woman who swallowed a cow,
I wonder how she swallowed a cow?
She swallowed the cow to catch the dog,
She swallowed the dog to catch the cat,
She swallowed the cat to catch the bird,
She swallowed the bird to catch the spider
That wriggled and jiggled and tickled inside her.
She swallowed the spider to catch the fly,
I don't know why she swallowed a fly,
Perhaps she'll die!

There was an old woman who
swallowed A HORSE.
She's dead, of course!

22 April • I Went to the River • Anon.

The old woman who swallowed a fly isn't the only bad decision-maker to be found in nursery rhymes. We continue with a brief run about poor choices – this one concerns itself with money matters.

I went to the river
And couldn't get across,
Paid five dollars
For an old gray hoss.

The horse wouldn't pull,
So I traded for a bull;

The bull wouldn't holler,
So I traded for a dollar;

The dollar wouldn't pass,
So I throwed it in the grass;

The grass wouldn't grow,
So I traded for a hoe;

The hoe wouldn't dig,
So I traded for a pig;

The pig wouldn't squeal,
So I traded for a wheel;

The wheel wouldn't run,
So I traded for a gun;

The gun wouldn't shoot,
So I traded for a boot;

The boot wouldn't fit,
So I thought I'd better quit.

23 April • Old Mother Hubbard • Sarah Catherine Martin

The long version of this nursery rhyme is credited to Sarah Catherine Martin (1768–1826) who published it in 1805. By the following year, it was so popular that commentators began complaining about the public doting on it – almost like an early 'Baby Shark' song (see 14 August).

Old Mother Hubbard
Went to the cupboard
To get her poor dog a bone;
But when she got there,
The cupboard was bare,
And so the poor dog had none.

She went to the baker's
To buy him some bread,
And when she came back
The poor dog was dead.

She went to the joiner's
To buy him a coffin,
But when she came back
The poor dog was laughing.

She took a clean dish
To get him some tripe,
But when she came back
He was smoking his pipe.

She went to the fishmonger's
  To buy him some fish,
And when she came back
  He was washing the dish.

She went to the ale-house
  To get him some beer,
But when she came back
  The dog sat in a chair.

She went to the tavern
  For white wine and red,
But when she came back
  The dog stood on his head.

She went to the hatter's
  To buy him a hat,
But when she came back
  He was feeding the cat.

She went to the barber's
  To buy him a wig,
But when she came back
  He was dancing a jig.

She went to the fruiterer's
  To buy him some fruit,
But when she came back
  He was playing the flute.

She went to the tailor's
    To buy him a coat,
And when she came back
    He was riding a goat.

She went to the cobbler's
    To buy him some shoes,
And when she came back
    He was reading the news.

She went to the sempstress
   To buy him some linen,
But when she came back
   The dog was spinning.

She went to the hosier's
   To buy him some hose,
But when she came back
   He was dressed in his clothes.

The dame made a curtsy,
   The dog made a bow,
The dame said, 'Your servant,'
   The dog said, 'Bow, wow.'

24 April • I Sold Me a Horse • Anon.

Finally, bad trades reach the level of the truly disastrous in today's entry.

I sold me a horse
    And bought me a cow,
I tried to make bargains
    But I didn't know how.

I sold me a cow
    And bought me a calf,
I tried to make bargains
    But always lost half.

I sold me a calf
    And bought me a swine,
He couldn't chew corn,
    For his teeth were too fine.

I sold me a swine
    And bought me a hen,
She laid eggs,
    But the devil knew when.

I sold me a hen
    And bought me a cock,
He never crowed
    Till nine o'clock.

I sold me a cock
    And bought me a rat,
His tail caught a-fire,
    And burned my old hat.

I sold me a rat
    And bought me a mouse,
His tail caught fire
    And burned my old house.

25 April • There Was an Old Crow • Anon.

Although often associated with fairy tales, many nursery rhymes actually take pains to avoid telling stories. This one is traditionally used by reluctant singers when asked to perform, but it also exists in an alternate version for people who dislike public speaking, where the ending is 'And now my sermon is ended / Thank God.'

There was an old crow
Sat upon a clod;
That's the end of my song. –
That's odd.

26 April • Three Wise Men of Gotham • Anon.

Another rhyme that tries to avoid telling lengthy stories refers to the village of Gotham, near Nottingham, in England. Between the Middle Ages and the mid-1800s, Gotham was famous for the supposed stupidity of its inhabitants; a different place to the fictional city protected by Batman many years later.

Three wise men of Gotham
Went to sea in a bowl:
And if the bowl had been stronger,
My song would have been longer.

27 April • Betty Botter • Carolyn Wells

Try to wrap your tongue around these two slippery sentences.

Betty Botter bought some butter,
But, she said, this butter's bitter;
If I put it in my batter,
It will make my batter bitter,
But a bit of better butter
Will make my batter better.
So she bought a bit of butter
Better than her bitter butter,
And she put it in her batter,
And it made her batter better,
So 'twas better Betty Botter
Bought a bit of better butter.

28 April • Peter Piper Picked a Peck of Pickled Pepper • Anon.

Our next tongue-twister is supposed to cure the hiccups if you can say it three times without taking a breath.

> Peter Piper picked a peck of pickled pepper;
> A peck of pickled pepper Peter Piper picked;
> If Peter Piper picked a peck of pickled pepper,
> Where's the peck of pickled pepper Peter Piper picked?

29 April • Moses Supposes his Toeses are Roses • Anon.

This tongue-torturing rhyme makes a famous appearance in a tap-dancing sequence in the MGM hit movie *Singin' in the Rain* (1952).

> Moses supposes his toeses are roses;
> But Moses supposes erroneously;
> For nobody's toeses are posies of roses,
> As Moses supposes his toeses to be.

30 April • How Much Wood Could a Woodchuck Chuck? • Anon.

A woodchuck is otherwise known as a groundhog; a baby groundhog is known as a chuckling.

How much wood could a woodchuck chuck
If a woodchuck could chuck wood?
As much wood as a woodchuck could chuck
If a woodchuck could chuck wood!

May Day, Farm, Market, London

1 May • The Fair Maid who, the First of May • Anon.

May Day falls halfway between the spring equinox and the summer solstice. The earliest known May Day celebrations date back to the Roman Republic (509 BC–27 BC), with the Festival of Flora – the Roman goddess of flowers. Traditional activities, many of which take place today, include gathering wildflowers, weaving garlands and dancing around a maypole. This rhyme describes one of many superstitions about the holiday, which is associated with the hawthorn tree. In England, the hawthorn is actually known as the May tree, because it blossoms at this time of year.

The fair maid who, the first of May,
Goes to the fields at break of day,
And washes in dew from the hawthorn tree,
Will ever after handsome be.

2 May • A Swarm of Bees in May • Anon.

Beekeepers' calendars are the subject of today's rhyme. Bees swarm between spring and summer as they leave their hives to seek new ones, and beekeepers take advantage of this by establishing new hives between May and June. By July, though, it is too late. May bees are worth less than June bees, as the rhyme indicates, because their honey is lighter, blander, and quicker to harden.

A swarm of bees in May
Is worth a load of hay.

A swarm of bees in June
Is worth a silver spoon.

A swarm of bees in July
Is not even worth a fly.

3 May • Here We Go Gathering Nuts in May • Anon.

This May rhyme is associated with a children's tug-of-war game. The children stand in two lines facing each other; one line skips towards the other and sings the first verse, then the other line skips forward singing the second. The children whose names are chosen stand in the middle for a game of tug-of-war, and the loser has to join the opposing line.

Here we go gathering nuts in May,
Nuts in May, nuts in May,
Here we go gathering nuts in May,
On a cold and frosty morning.

Who will you have for nuts in May,
Nuts in May, nuts in May,
Who will you have for nuts in May,
On a cold and frosty morning?

We'll have *Rosie* for nuts in May,
Nuts in May, nuts in May,
We'll have *Rosie* for nuts in May,
On a cold and frosty morning.

Who will you have to pull her away,
Pull her away, pull her away,
Who will you have to pull her away,
On a cold and frosty morning?

We'll have *Eliza* to pull her away,
Pull her away, pull her away.
We'll have *Eliza* to pull her away,
On a cold and frosty morning.

4 May • Mary, Mary, Quite Contrary • Anon.

May is a month for enjoying an abundance of new flora and fauna. This well-known garden rhyme has been around since at least the mid-eighteenth century. Like many other nursery rhymes, it has been interpreted variously, with some giving it religious significance.

Mary, Mary, quite contrary,
  How does your garden grow?
With silver bells and cockle shells,
  And pretty maids all in a row.

5 May • Noisy Garden • Julia Donaldson

This floral rhyme comes from the imagination of Julia Donaldson.

If tiger lilies and dandelions growled,
And cowslips mooed, and dog roses howled,
And snapdragons roared and catmint miaowed,
My garden would be extremely loud.

6 May • Creepy Crawlies • Rod Campbell

Today's garden rhyme is by another much-loved contemporary author: this time, Rod Campbell, creator of the classic lift-the-flap book *Dear Zoo* (1982). In this rhyme he encourages us to go and explore the world outdoors.

Little creatures live in trees,
Hiding away under leaves;
Very small and hard to see,
They crawl about, quietly.
Go on now, lift a leaf –
See what's sitting underneath.

7 May • Ladybird, Ladybird • Anon.

Here's a nursery rhyme to recite when a ladybird lands on a child's finger. The custom is that if you recite it to a ladybird and then blow on it once, it will fly away. It nearly always works . . .

Ladybird, ladybird,
  Fly away home,
Your house is on fire,
  And your children all gone;
All except one
  And that's little Ann
And she has crept under
  The warming pan.

8 May • The Ugly Duckling • Frank Loesser

Frank Loesser (1910–1969), the American songwriter of 'Baby, It's Cold Outside' fame, wrote this song for the musical film *Hans Christian Andersen* (1952), to be performed by the American star Danny Kaye.

There once was an ugly duckling
With feathers all stubby and brown
And the other birds said, in so many words,
Get out of town
Get out, get out, get out of town.

And he went with a quack and a waddle and a quack
In a flurry of eiderdown.

That poor little ugly duckling
Went wandering far and near
But at every place they said to his face
Now get out of here,
Get out, get out of here.

And he went with a quack and a waddle and a quack
And a very unhappy tear.

All through the wintertime he hid himself away
Ashamed to show his face, afraid of what others might say
All through the winter in his lonely clump of wheat
Till a flock of swans spied him there and very soon agreed,

You're a very fine swan indeed!
A swan? Me a swan? Ah, go on!
And he said yes, you're a swan
Take a look at yourself in the lake and you'll see
And he looked, and he saw, and he said
Why it's me!
I am a swan! Wheeeeeeee!

I'm not such an ugly duckling
No feathers all stubby and brown
For in fact these birds in so many words said
The best in town,
The best, the best, the best in town.

Not a quack, not a quack, not a waddle or a quack
But a glide and a whistle and a snowy white back
And a head so noble and high
Say, who's an ugly duckling?
Not I!
Not I!

9 May • Dingle-Dangle Scarecrow • Anon.

Moving on from the garden to the farm, here is a delightful rhyme about scarecrows – featuring far more activity than you might expect, given that a scarecrow is traditionally inanimate!

When all the cows were sleeping
And the sun had gone to bed
Up jumped the scarecrow
And this is what he said:

I'm a dingle-dangle scarecrow
With a flippy-floppy hat
I can shake my hands like this
And shake my feet like that!

When all the hens were roosting
And the moon behind the cloud
Up jumped the scarecrow
And shouted very loud:

I'm a dingle-dangle scarecrow
With a flippy-floppy hat
I can shake my hands like this
And shake my feet like that!

When the dogs were in the kennels
And the doves were in the loft
Up jumped the scarecrow
And whispered very soft:

I'm a dingle-dangle scarecrow
With a flippy-floppy hat
I can shake my hands like this
And shake my feet like that.

I'm a dingle-dangle scarecrow
With a flippy-floppy hat
I can shake my hands like this
And shake my feet like that.

10 May • In and Out the Dusty Bluebells • Anon.

'In and Out the Dusty Bluebells' is accompanied by a circle game. The children stand in a circle with their hands above their heads to form arches of 'dusty bluebells', and the first player dances in and out of the arches. Wherever they stop, they tap the shoulder of the person in front of them to be the 'master'; the group then sings it again, with the master joining the first player to dance. This continues until everyone is weaving in and out of an imaginary circle, or has collapsed with exhaustion.

In and out the dusty bluebells,
In and out the dusty bluebells,
In and out the dusty bluebells,
Who shall be my master?

Tippitty tappitty on your shoulder,
Tippitty tappitty on your shoulder,
Tippitty tappitty on your shoulder,
You shall be my master.

11 May • Oats and Beans and Barley Grow • Anon.

This is another circle game, speculated to have origins in a spring fertility chant. To play the game, children sit in a circle around the 'farmer', who must act out sowing, stamping and clapping. The farmer picks a 'wife' and together they stand in the circle, pretending to chop wood.

Oats and beans and barley grow,
Oats and beans and barley grow.
Do you or I or anyone know
How oats and beans and barley grow?

First the farmer sows his seed,
Then he stands and takes his ease,
Stamps his foot, and claps his hand,
And turns around to view the land.

Waiting for a partner,
Waiting for a partner,
Waiting for a partner,
So open the ring and let one in.

Now you're married you must obey,
You must be true to all you say;
You must be kind, you must be good,
And help your wife to chop the wood.
Chop it thin and carry it in,
And kiss your partner in the ring.

12 May • The Farmer's in his Den • Anon.

Football fans have reworked this rhyme to chant 'We've won the cup, we've won the cup, ee-aye-addio, we've won the cup', with extra verses often made up on the spot. It is famous as the song fans sang when England won the World Cup in 1966.

The farmer's in his den,
The farmer's in his den,
Ee-aye-addio,
The farmer's in his den.

The farmer wants a wife,
The farmer wants a wife,
Ee-aye-addio,
The farmer wants a wife.

The wife wants a child,
The wife wants a child,
Ee-aye-addio,
The wife wants a child.

The child wants a nurse,
The child wants a nurse,
Ee-aye-addio,
The child wants a nurse.

The nurse wants a dog,
The nurse wants a dog,
Ee-aye-addio,
The nurse wants a dog.

The dog wants a bone,
The dog wants a bone,
Ee-aye-addio,
The dog wants a bone.

We all pat the bone,
We all pat the bone,
Ee-aye-addio,
We all pat the bone.

13 May • Old Macdonald had a Farm • Anon.

Another rhyme often appropriated as a football chant traces its roots to part of a 'comick Opera' by Thomas D'Urfey (1653–1723), *Wonders in the Sun, or the Kingdom of the Birds* (1706). (You can have fun adding different animals into the verses – and making all the noises.)

Old Macdonald had a farm
E-I-E-I-O.
And on that farm he had some cows
E-I-E-I-O.
With a moo-moo here,
And a moo-moo there,
Here a moo, there a moo,
Everywhere a moo-moo,
Old Macdonald had a farm,
E-I-E-I-O.

Old Macdonald had a farm,
E-I-E-I-O
And on that farm he had some sheep,
E-I-E-I-O.
    With a baa-baa here,
    And a baa-baa there,
    Here a baa, there a baa,
    Everywhere a baa-baa,
Old Macdonald had a farm,
E-I-E-I-O.

Old Macdonald had a farm,
E-I-E-I-O
And on that farm he had some hens,
E-I-E-I-O.
    With a cluck-cluck here,
    And a cluck-cluck there,
    Here a cluck, there a cluck,
    Everywhere a cluck-cluck,
Old Macdonald had a farm,
E-I-E-I-O.

14 May • There Was a Farmer had a Dog • Anon.

Here is another traditional farm rhyme, this one dating back to its first known printing in 1780. It is often sung to an extremely catchy tune – which has been left out here in order to preserve parents' sanity.

There was a farmer had a dog,
And Bingo was his name-o.
  B-I-N-G-O!
  B-I-N-G-O!
  B-I-N-G-O!
And Bingo was his name-o!

There was a farmer had a dog,
And Bingo was his name-o.
  (*Clap*)-I-N-G-O!
  (*Clap*)-I-N-G-O!
  (*Clap*)-I-N-G-O!
And Bingo was his name-o!

There was a farmer had a dog,
And Bingo was his name-o.
  (*Clap, clap*)-N-G-O!
  (*Clap, clap*)-N-G-O!
  (*Clap, clap*)-N-G-O!
And Bingo was his name-o!

There was a farmer had a dog,
And Bingo was his name-o.
    (*Clap, clap, clap*)-G-O!
    (*Clap, clap, clap*)-G-O!
    (*Clap, clap, clap*)-G-O!
And Bingo was his name-o!

There was a farmer had a dog,
And Bingo was his name-o.
    (*Clap, clap, clap, clap*)-O!
    (*Clap, clap, clap, clap*)-O!
    (*Clap, clap, clap, clap*)-O!
And Bingo was his name-o!

There was a farmer had a dog,
And Bingo was his name-o.
    (*Clap, clap, clap, clap, clap*)
    (*Clap, clap, clap, clap, clap*)
    (*Clap, clap, clap, clap, clap*)
And Bingo was his name-o!

15 May • The Cow • Robert Louis Stevenson

The Scottish writer Robert Louis Stevenson (1850–1894) is best known for his novels *Treasure Island* and *Strange Case of Dr Jekyll and Mr Hyde*, but he also wrote an extremely successful book of poems for young children, *A Child's Garden of Verses*, from which this has been taken.

The friendly cow all red and white
  I love with all my heart:
She gives me cream with all her might,
  To eat with apple-tart.

She wanders lowing here and there,
  And yet she cannot stray,
All in the pleasant open air,
  The pleasant light of day;

And blown by all the winds that pass
  And wet with all the showers,
She walks among the meadow grass
  And eats the meadow flowers.

16 May • Goosey, Goosey, Gander • Anon.

Old men are often unlucky in nursery rhymes, and today's entry is no exception. Some have speculated that it was originally about some form of religious persecution.

Goosey, goosey, gander,
    Whither shall I wander?
Upstairs and downstairs
    And in my lady's chamber.

There I met an old man
    That wouldn't say his prayers;
I took him by the left leg,
    And threw him down the stairs.

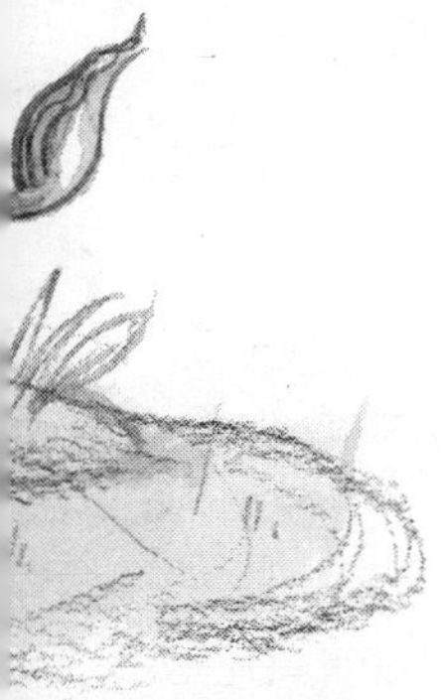

17 May • Old Mother Goose • Anon.

Mother Goose (or in France, Mère l'Oye) is a legendary figure who rode on the back of a flying gander to collect sayings, chants, folksongs and lullabies which we now call . . . nursery rhymes! In verses 11 and 12, Harlequin and Columbine are the stock comic servant lovers from the *commedia dell'arte* Italian theatre.

Old Mother Goose,
When she wanted to wander,
Would ride through the air
On a very fine gander.

Mother Goose had a house,
'Twas built in a wood,
Where an owl at the door
For sentinel stood.

She had a son Jack,
A plain-looking lad,
He was not very good,
Nor yet very bad.

She sent him to market,
A live goose he bought;
'Here, Mother,' says he,
'It will not go for naught.'

Jack's goose and her gander
Grew very fond,
They'd both eat together,
Or swim in one pond.

Jack found one morning,
    As I have been told,
His goose had laid him
    An egg of pure gold.

Jack rode to his mother,
    The news for to tell;
She called him a good boy,
    And said it was well.

Jack sold his gold egg
    To a rogue and a cad,
Who stole half the proceeds
    Away from the lad.

Then Jack went a-courting
    A lady so gay,
As fair as the lily,
    And sweet as the May.

The rogue and the Squire
    Came behind his back,
And began to belabour
    The sides of poor Jack.

But Old Mother Goose
    That instant came in,
And turned her son Jack
    Into famed Harlequin.

She then with her wand
    Touched the lady so fine,

And turned her at once
Into sweet Columbine.

The gold egg into the sea
Was thrown then –
When Jack jumped in,
And got the egg back again.

The rogue got the goose,
Which he vowed he would kill,
Resolving at once
His pockets to fill.

Jack's mother came in,
And caught the goose soon,
And mounting its back,
Flew up to the moon.

18 May • Leg Over Leg • Anon.

This sprightly rhyme is typically recited to small children as they sit, facing outwards, on an adult's knee. The adult criss-crosses the child's ankles to the beat of the rhyme, then lifts them into the air on 'JUMP!'

Leg over leg,
As the dog went to Dover.
When he came to a stile,
JUMP! He went over.

19 May • Ding, Dong, Bell • Anon.

This nursery rhyme was first printed in 1609, but was already considered old. Two of Shakespeare's plays seem to refer to the nursery rhyme, in each case as part of a song. In *The Merchant of Venice* (Act 3, Scene 2) we find the couplet, 'Let us all ring fancy's knell; / I'll begin it – Ding, dong, bell'; and Ariel's song in *The Tempest* (Act 1, Scene 2) uses the very same rhyme: 'Sea-nymphs hourly ring his knell: / Hark! Now I hear them – Ding, dong, bell!'

Ding, dong, bell,
Pussy's in the well!
Who put her in?
Little Johnny Green.
Who pulled her out?
Little Tommy Stout.
What a naughty boy was that
To try to drown poor pussy-cat,
Who never did him any harm,
But killed the mouse in his father's barn.

20 May • Tom, He Was a Piper's Son • Anon.

The phrase 'over the hills and far away' has been described as one of the most beautiful lines in English poetry. The nineteenth-century poets Robert Burns and Robert Louis Stevenson made the line their own – as has Rod Campbell in more recent times (see 13 July).

Tom, he was a piper's son,
He learnt to play when he was young,
And all the tune that he could play
Was 'Over the hills and far away'.
    Over the hills and a great way off,
    The wind shall blow my top-knot off.

Tom with his pipe made such a noise,
That he pleased both the girls and boys,
They all danced while he did play,
'Over the hills and far away'.
    Over the hills and a great way off,
    The wind shall blow my top-knot off.

Tom with his pipe did play with such skill
That those who heard him could never keep still;
As soon as he played they began for to dance,
Even pigs on their hind legs would after him prance.
    Over the hills and a great way off,
    The wind shall blow my top-knot off.

As Dolly was milking her cow one day,
Tom took his pipe and began for to play;
So Dolly and the cow danced 'The Cheshire Round',
Till the pail was broken and the milk ran on the ground.
    Over the hills and a great way off,
    The wind shall blow my top-knot off.

He met old Dame Trot with a basket of eggs,
He used his pipe and she used her legs;
She danced about till the eggs were all broke,
She began for to fret, but he laughed at the joke.
    Over the hills and a great way off,
    The wind shall blow my top-knot off.

Tom saw a cross fellow was beating an ass,
Heavy laden with pots, pans, dishes, and glass;
He took out his pipe and he played them a tune,
And the poor donkey's load was lightened full soon.
    Over the hills and a great way off,
    The wind shall blow my top-knot off.

21 May • This Little Pig went to Market • Anon.

Now we move from farmers' fields to farmers' markets with a well-known fingerplay. This nursery rhyme is accompanied by counting a toddler's fingers or toes (if you can get them to sit still) and was repurposed in the early twentieth century to help the Suffragette cause (see 9 March).

This little pig went to market,
This little pig stayed at home,
This little pig had roast beef,
This little pig had none,
And this little pig cried, 'Wee-wee-wee!'
    All the way home.

22 May • To Market, to Market, to Buy a Fat Pig • Anon.

Today's market rhyme is referenced in the science-fiction film *Blade Runner* (1982), in which a prematurely ageing planetary exile is taunted by the genetically engineered companions he has created with the old-fashioned and nostalgic phrase, 'Home again, home again, jiggety-jig'.

To market, to market, to buy a fat pig;
  Home again, home again, jiggety-jig,
To market, to market, to buy a fat hog;
  Home again, home again, jiggety-jog.

23 May • Highty Cock O! • Anon

We leave the market and head now to London for a run of rhymes beginning with this jaunty sexain (six-liner), which was collected by James Orchard Halliwell-Phillipps (1820–1889) for his book, *The Nursery Rhymes of England* (1842).

Highty Cock O!
To London we go,
To York we ride;
And Edward has pussy-cat tied to his side;
He shall have little dog tied to the other;
And then he goes trid-trod to see his grandmother.

24 May • See-Saw, Sacradown • Anon.

Around since before 1720 when it was quoted in a ballad, this is a rhyme to sing on a see-saw. A see-saw, easily constructed out of logs, is one of the oldest children's games.

> See-saw, sacradown,
> Which is the way to London Town?
> One foot up, the other foot down,
> That is the way to London Town.

25 May • London Bridge is Falling Down • Anon.

The classic nursery rhyme 'London Bridge is Falling Down', first recorded in this form in the seventeenth century, is perhaps the rhyme that has gone on to have the most success on Broadway and in Hollywood. The musical *My Fair Lady* (1956) took its title from the last line, the cockney pronunciation of 'Mayfair lady'.

> London Bridge is falling down,
>   Falling down, falling down,
> London Bridge is falling down,
>   My fair lady.
>
> Build it up with wood and clay,
>   Wood and clay, wood and clay,
> Build it up with wood and clay,
>   My fair lady.

Wood and clay will wash away,
Wash away, wash away,
Wood and clay will wash away,
My fair lady.

Build it up with bricks and mortar,
Bricks and mortar, bricks and mortar,
Build it up with bricks and mortar,
My fair lady.

Bricks and mortar will not stay,
Will not stay, will not stay,
Bricks and mortar will not stay,
My fair lady.

Build it up with iron and steel,
Iron and steel, iron and steel,
Build it up with iron and steel,
My fair lady.

Iron and steel will bend and bow,
Bend and bow, bend and bow,
Iron and steel will bend and bow,
My fair lady.

Build it up with silver and gold,
Silver and gold, silver and gold,
Build it up with silver and gold,
My fair lady.

Silver and gold will be stolen away,
Stolen away, stolen away,
Silver and gold will be stolen away,
My fair lady.

Set a man to watch all night,
    Watch all night, watch all night,
Set a man to watch all night,
    My fair lady.

Suppose the man should fall asleep,
    Fall asleep, fall asleep,
Suppose the man should fall asleep,
    My fair lady.

Give him a pipe to smoke all night,
    Smoke all night, smoke all night,
Give him a pipe to smoke all night,
    My fair lady.

26 May • Sir Christopher Wren • E. C. Bentley

Edmund Clerihew Bentley (1875–1956) gave us the 'clerihew', which are four-line poems where the first line names the poem's subject, usually someone famous, and the remaining three make light of their biography. Sir Christopher Wren (1632–1723), one of the most important architects in the London cityscape, is the unlucky subject of this example of the form.

Sir Christopher Wren
Said, 'I am going to dine with some men.
If anyone calls,
Say I am designing St Paul's.'

27 May • Oranges and Lemons • Anon.

To play the game associated with this eighteenth-century London rhyme, two people face each other holding their hands above their heads to form an archway or 'chopper'. While the rhyme is sung, the other players make their way through the archway until the 'chopper' traps someone on the last word, who is then out of the game. This grisly game has long been believed to represent the journey someone would take through London on their way to being executed, marking all the churches on their way.

St Clement's could be either the church of St Clement Danes in Westminster, or St Clement's Church in Eastcheap, both of which are close to fruit markets; St Martin's is on St Martin's Lane in the City of London, which used to be full of money lenders – hence owing five farthings. The Old Bailey is not itself a church, but England's central criminal court; the bell would ring to mark the execution of a prisoner of Newgate Gaol. Shoreditch Church is properly called St Leonard's, and the bells of Stepney are those of St Dunstan and All Saints Church, which was built in the Middle Ages. The great bell at Bow has also been there since the Middle Ages, erected in 1070 at St Mary-le-Bow church in Cheapside.

This rhyme has been referenced frequently and variously, from George Orwell's famous dystopian novel *Nineteen Eighty-Four* (1949) to Michael Morpurgo's beloved war novel *Private Peaceful* (2003) – and in lyrics by the London rock band The Clash.

Oranges and lemons,
Say the bells of St Clement's.

You owe me five farthings,
Say the bells of St Martin's.

When will you pay me?
Say the bells of Old Bailey.

When I grow rich,
Say the bells of Shoreditch.

When will that be?
Say the bells of Stepney.

I'm sure I don't know,
Says the great bell at Bow.

Here comes a candle to light you to bed,
Here comes a chopper to chop off your head.

28 May • Do You Know the Muffin Man? • Anon.

The first printing of this rhyme appears as 'The Dandy muffin-man of Drury Lane' in an 1819 manuscript in the British Library. There is sadly no evidence of the man's name, so despite generations of children singing the second verse, history has it that nobody knows the muffin man.

Do you know the muffin man
Do you know the muffin man
Do you know the muffin man
  Who lives in Drury Lane?

Yes, I know the muffin man
Yes, I know the muffin man
Yes, I know the muffin man
  Who lives in Drury Lane.

29 May • Pussy-cat, Pussy-cat, Where Have You Been? • Anon.

Although it was not recorded in print until 1805, this rhyme is widely believed to have first appeared in Tudor times, when one of Queen Elizabeth I's ladies-in-waiting had a cat who frightened a little mouse under the queen's throne.

> Pussy-cat, pussy-cat, where have you been?
> I've been up to London to look at the queen.
> Pussy-cat, pussy-cat, what did you there?
> I frightened a little mouse under the chair.

30 May • Half a Pound of Tuppenny Rice • Anon.

This is another London rhyme, from the 1850s: The Eagle is a pub on London's City Road, which today proudly bears the lines of the last stanza on its outside walls. There are many theories as to what the lyrics mean (if anything) – the most popular being that spending money at the 'Eagle' (pub) leads you to the pawnbrokers to 'pop' (pawn) your 'weasel' (coat).

Half a pound of tuppenny rice,
Half a pound of treacle.
That's the way the money goes,
Pop goes the weasel.

Every night when I go out,
The monkey's on the table,
Take a stick and knock it off,
Pop goes the weasel.

Up and down the City Road,
In and out the Eagle,
That's the way the money goes,
Pop goes the weasel.

31 May • It's Vesak! • Anon.

Finally, to end the month, we have a rhyme to celebrate Vesak. Vesak is a Buddhist festival that celebrates Buddha's birth, enlightenment and death. It takes place on the night of the full moon in the lunar month of Vaisakha (which usually falls in April or May).

It's Vesak!
The moon is out!
It's time to meditate,
Sing and celebrate!
The bells chime in
As the night begins;
Tinkles and gongs
Ring all night long!
It's Vesak!
It's Vesak!

The full moon,
In complete bloom,
Calls for a picnic night
Under the starry light.
The bells chime in
As the night begins;
Tinkles and gongs
Ring all night long!
It's Vesak!
It's Vesak!

Sometime in May,
Or June they say,
Comes the bright night,
It's a pretty sight.
The bells chime in
As the night begins;
Tinkles and gongs
Ring all night long!
It's Vesak!
It's Vesak!

It's Buddha's day,
Who showed us the way!
He was a great teacher,
Taught us how to live better.
The bells chime in
As the night begins;
Tinkles and gongs
Ring all night long!
It's Vesak!
It's Vesak!

Playground Games, Animals

1 June • Here Sits the Lord Mayor • Anon.

June begins with a run of rhymes to accompany the lengthening summer evenings. This traditional rhyme indicates – on each of its seven lines – which part of the child's face to touch or tickle.

Here sits the Lord Mayor, (*forehead*)
Here sit his men, (*eyes*)
Here sits the cockadoodle, (*left cheek*)
Here sits the hen, (*right cheek*)
Here sit the little chickens, (*tip of nose*)
Here they run in, (*mouth*)
Chin chopper, chin chopper, chin chopper, chin.
(*tickle under chin*)

2 June • See-Saw, Margery Daw • Anon.

This is our second rhyme that accompanies a ride on a see-saw (see 24 May). 'Margery Daw' was probably not a real person but simply invented for rhyming with 'see-saw'. The rhyme appears as early as 1788 and Tommy's situation might be referring to the trials and tribulations of child labour in a workhouse.

See-saw, Margery Daw,
Tommy shall have a new master,
He shall have but a penny a day,
Because he can't work any faster.

3 June • I'm a Little Girl Scout • Anon.

Skipping-rope or jumping-rope chants go back at least as early as the eighteenth century. This is a skipping rhyme, which some people know as 'I'm a Little Dutch Girl', rather than 'Girl Scout'. The skipper performs the 'actions', and succeeds in the game if they can count to sixteen without being caught by the rope.

I'm a little girl scout, dressed in blue,
Here are the actions I must do.
Salute to the captain,
Bow to the Queen,
Turn right round
And count sixteen.
One, two, three . . . sixteen.

4 June • Skipping Rhyme • Brian Bilston

Today's entry is a brand-new skipping rhyme, given to us by the poet Brian Bilston (whom we met on 6 January).

1-2-3-4
Pick your feet up off the _____
5-6-7-8
Don't jump too soon or jump too _____
9-10-11-12
Be careful not to hurt your _____
13-14-through the teens
If you don't know what this all _____
20 up to 51
And wonder where some words have _____
52 to 99
It's because this song keeps skipping _____

5 June • Granny in the Kitchen • Anon.

In this skipping rhyme from Belfast, grandmothers come in for attention again (see 23 May).

Granny in the kitchen
    Doing a bit of stitchin'.
In comes a bogeyman
    And chases Granny out.
'Oh!' says Granny.
    'That's not fair!'
'Oh!' says the bogeyman.
    'I don't care.'

6 June • Down in the Valley • Anon.

To play the game associated with this rhyme, children make a circle with one person in the middle, whose name is used in the third line. They then invite someone else into the middle to pretend to have tea with them while the last verse is sung.

Down in the valley
    Where the green grass grows,
There stands *Eliza*,
    Washing out her clothes.
She sang and she sang
    And she sang so sweet,
She sang for her playmate
    Across the street.

Rosie, *Rosie*,
    Will you come to tea?
Come next Saturday
    At half past three.
Tea, cakes, pancakes,
    All for you and me.
Won't we have a lovely time
    At half past three.

7 June • Lou, Lou, Skip to Me Lou • Anon.

Famously recorded by both Nat King Cole and Judy Garland, this traditional rhyme is used in a simple game of swapping partners while square dancing. It has also been adapted by football fans who, for example, sang this about the former Manchester United player Lou Macari: 'Skip to me, Lou Macari!' In the original, 'lou' is a corruption of 'loo' – a Scots word for 'love'.

Lou, lou, skip to me lou,
Lou, lou, skip to me lou,
Lou, lou, skip to me lou,
    Skip to me lou, my darling.

Lost my partner, what shall I do?
Lost my partner, what shall I do?
Lost my partner, what shall I do?
    Skip to me lou, my darling.

I've found another one, just like you,
I've found another one, just like you,
I've found another one, just like you,
    Skip to me lou, my darling.

8 June • Charley, Charley, Stole the Barley • Anon.

From the late nineteenth century we have a cautionary rhyme about petty theft.

Charley, Charley,
Stole the barley
Out of the baker's shop,
The baker came out
And gave him a clout,
Which made poor Charley hop.

9 June • Ipper Dipper Dation • Anon.

Today's rhyme doubles as a tool for helping children pick who will be 'it' in their game. A popular variant is, 'Ip dip sky blue / Who's it? Not you!'

Ipper dipper dation,
My operation.
How many people at the station?
The one who comes to number . . . five
Will surely not be IT.
One, two, three, four, five.

10 June • Eenie, Meenie, Mackeracka • Anon.

Counting-out or 'you're it' rhymes are full of nonsense words as the rhyme merely serves to accompany the action. According to English folklore, these seemingly innocent games are relics of the formulae that ancient Druids used when choosing human sacrifices! I wonder if Rihanna knew this when quoting these words in her song 'Raining Men'.

Eenie, meenie, mackeracka,
Hi, di, dominacka,
Stickeracka, roomeracka,
Om, pom, push.

11 June • Hanna, Manna, Mona, Mike • Anon.

Hopefully with a less sinister origin, this counting out rhyme can be traced back to New York in 1815, so it was unlikely to have been used by any Druids.

Hanna, Manna, Mona, Mike
Barcelona, Bona, Strike
Harry, Warry, Frown, Venack
Harrico, Warrico
Wee, Wo, Whack
You're IT!

12 June • Here is the Church, and Here is the Steeple • Anon.

Building up to a run of clapping games, here is a simple (though hard to explain!) finger game, so bear with me. You start with the tops of your fingers interlocked, knuckles outwards, and raise your two little fingers to represent a steeple. Then, by turning your hands inside out you can reveal the people (represented by the fingertips). For the parson to go upstairs, you intertwine your fingers one by one, and then on 'prayers' clap your hands together flat, as though praying. Good luck!

Here is the church, and here is the steeple;
Open the door and here are the people.
Here is the parson going upstairs,
And here he is a-saying his prayers.

13 June • Pat-a-Cake, Pat-a-Cake, Baker's Man • Anon.

'Pat-a-Cake' first appeared in another one of Thomas D'Urfey's comedies, *The Campaigners* (1698). Singers of this clapping rhyme over time have replaced the 'B' for 'Baby' with the initial and name of the child they are singing to. Pricking a cake with an identifiable mark harks back to a time when most households did not have their own kitchen, and ingredients were taken to a bake house – essentially a communal oven.

> Pat-a-cake, pat-a-cake, baker's man,
> Bake me a cake as fast as you can;
> Pat it and prick it, and mark it with B,
> And put it in the oven for Baby and me.

14 June • If You're Happy and You Know it, Clap Your Hands • Anon.

You might hear this song reworked by crowds at football matches, perhaps best adapted by Newcastle United's fans about former player Peter Løvenkrands: 'If you're happy and you know it, Løvenkrands.'

If you're happy and you know it, clap your hands.
If you're happy and you know it, clap your hands.
If you're happy and you know it, and you really want to show it,
If you're happy and you know it, clap your hands.

If you're happy and you know it, stamp your feet.
If you're happy and you know it, stamp your feet.
If you're happy and you know it, and you really want to show it,
If you're happy and you know it, stamp your feet.

If you're happy and you know it, nod your head.
If you're happy and you know it, nod your head.
If you're happy and you know it, and you really want to show it,
If you're happy and you know it, nod your head.

If you're happy and you know it, shout 'Hooray!'
If you're happy and you know it, shout 'Hooray!'
If you're happy and you know it, and you really want to show it,
If you're happy and you know it, shout 'Hooray!'

15 June • Two Little Dicky Birds • Anon.

Moving on from clapping games, here is a fingerplay to begin a run of nursery rhymes about birds. Small children are often delighted by this simple game, in which the speaker uses one hand to represent Peter and the other hand for Paul. When each bird flies away, the speaker hides their hand until the birds 'come back'.

Two little dicky birds,
Sitting on a wall;
One named Peter,
The other named Paul.
Fly away, Peter!
Fly away, Paul!
Come back, Peter!
Come back, Paul!

16 June • The Singing Bird • Anon.

'The Singing Bird' is a song that hails from Tennessee, USA. Songbirds are unique in that they actually learn, practise and perfect their songs – other birds know their calls from birth.

I saw a redbird in the air,
A redbird in a tree,
But a redbird in a bramble bush
Was the one that sang to me.
    Birdie, birdie in the air,
    Birdie in the tree!
    But the birdie I like best of all
    Is the one that sings to me!

I saw a blackbird in the air,
A blackbird in a tree,
But a blackbird in a bramble bush
Was the one that sang to me.
    Birdie, birdie in the air,
    Birdie in the tree!
    But the birdie I like best of all
    Is the one that sings to me!

I saw a bluebird in the air,
A bluebird in a tree,
But a bluebird in a bramble bush
Was the one that sang to me.
  Birdie, birdie in the air,
  Birdie in the tree!
  But the birdie I like best of all
  Is the one that sings to me!

17 June • A Little Cock Sparrow Sat on a Green Tree • Anon.

A cock sparrow is not actually a real sparrow, but a weaver finch – but never tell that to their face.

A little cock sparrow sat on a green tree,
And he chirruped, he chirruped, so merry was he.
A naughty boy came with his wee bow and arrow,
Says he, I will shoot this little cock sparrow.
His body will make me a nice little stew,
And his giblets will make me a little pie too.
'Oh, no,' said the sparrow, 'I won't make a stew,'
So he clapped his wings and away he flew.

18 June • All the Chi Chi Birds they Sing till Dawn • Anon.

This avian lullaby hails from Jamaica, the only place in the world where you can find a 'Doctor Bird' (or swallow-tail hummingbird).

All the chi chi birds they sing till dawn.
When the daylight comes all the birds are gone.
Chi, chi, chi, chi, chi, chi, what a pretty song.
This is what the birds are singing all night long.
Bam chi chi bam, they sing-a this song,
Bam chi chi bam, sing all the night long.
Bam chi chi bam, then just before day,
Bam chi chi bam, they fly away.

19 June • Once I Saw a Little Bird • Anon.

As in the previous few rhymes, today's entry highlights birds' elusiveness.

Once I saw a little bird
 Come *hop, hop, hop,*
So I cried, 'Little bird,
 Will you stop, stop, stop?'

I was going to the window
 To say 'How do you do?'
But he shook his little tail
 And away he flew.

20 June • The Robin and the Wren • Anon.

The following two rhymes illustrate that birds are often the subject of superstitions. This one warns children not to steal eggs from birds' nests.

The robin and the redbreast,
  The robin and the wren,
If you take them out of their nest,
  Ye'll ne'er thrive again.

The robin and the redbreast,
  The martin and the swallow;
If you touch one of their eggs,
  Ill luck is sure to follow.

21 June • One for Sorrow, Two for Joy • Anon.

The magpie is the subject of many different superstitions. Some say that seeing a single magpie brings bad luck and to reverse this bad luck, you must either cross your feet, raise your hat, spit at the bird while announcing 'I spit on thee, brother', say 'Good morning, Mr Magpie' but only if it is before noon, or make the sign of the cross while reciting: 'I cross the magpie / The magpie crosses me / Bad luck to the magpie / And good luck to me.' The RSPB would not encourage any of these acts. Alternatively, this rhyme acts as a fortune-teller as you count up all the magpies in view.

One for sorrow, two for joy,
Three for a girl and four for a boy,
Five for silver, six for gold,
Seven for a secret never to be told,
Eight for a letter over the sea,
Nine for a lover as true as can be.

22 June • Little Trotty Wagtail • John Clare

The great nature poet John Clare (1793–1864) gives us this delightful poem about a bird who is sometimes mistaken for a magpie: the wagtail. Often to be found in England, near a watery habitat, the wagtail is characterised by its long wagging tail.

Little trotty wagtail, he went in the rain,
And tittering, tottering sideways he ne'er got straight again.
He stooped to get a worm, and looked up to catch a fly,
And then he flew away ere his feathers they were dry.

Little trotty wagtail, he waddled in the mud,
And left his little footmarks, trample where he would.
He waddled in the water-pudge, and waggle went his tail,
And chirrupt up his wings to dry upon the garden rail.

Little trotty wagtail, you nimble all about,
And in the dimpling water-pudge you waddle in and out;
Your home is nigh at hand, and in the warm pigsty,
So, little Master Wagtail, I'll bid you a goodbye.

23 June • Sing a Song of Sixpence • Anon.

Thought to have been around since the 1500s, this British nursery rhyme might be referenced in Shakespeare's *Twelfth Night* (c. 1602) in the line, 'Whoa, here's a stir now! Sing a song o' sixpence!' and was adapted as the title of Agatha Christie's novel *A Pocket Full of Rye* (1953). For other things baked in pies, see 23 December.

Sing a song of sixpence,
A pocket full of rye;
Four and twenty blackbirds
Baked in a pie.

When the pie was opened,
The birds began to sing;
Was not that a dainty dish
To set before the king?

The king was in his counting-house
    Counting out his money;
The queen was in the parlour
    Eating bread and honey;

The maid was in the garden
    Hanging out the clothes,
There came a little blackbird,
    And snapped off her nose.

24 June • Hickory, Dickory, Dock • Anon.

Mice put in cameos in these following few nursery rhymes. In nineteenth-century Edinburgh, this rhyme was used by children to decide who should take the first turn in games, and it is known to have been a favourite of Sir Walter Scott. Since then, it has provided the title for the 1955 novel *Hickory Hickory Dock* by Agatha Christie (who was clearly a nursery rhyme superfan), in which she writes, ' "Hickory, dickory, dock," said Nigel, "the mouse ran up the clock. The police said, 'Boo,' I wonder who, will eventually stand in the Dock?" '

Hickory, Dickory, Dock,
The mouse ran up the clock;
    The clock struck one;
    The mouse ran down;
Hickory, Dickory, Dock.

25 June • Three Blind Mice • Anon.

'Three Blind Mice' seems to have been Agatha Christie's favourite nursery rhyme; aside from providing the title to *Three Blind Mice and Other Stories* (1950), it is an important theme in her murder mystery play *The Mousetrap* (1952) – don't worry: there are no spoilers!

Three blind mice, three blind mice,
See how they run, see how they run,
They all ran after the farmer's wife,
She cut off their tails with a carving knife;
Did you ever see such a thing in your life
    As three blind mice?

26 June • The Little Mouse • Anon.

Unlike the blade-wielding farmer's wife in yesterday's entry, the speaker of this poem tries to help the little mouse.

I have seen you, little mouse,
Running all about the house,
Through the hole, your little eye
In the wainscot peeping sly,
Hoping soon some crumbs to steal,
To make quite a hearty meal.
Look before you venture out,
See if pussy is about,
If she's gone, you'll quickly run
To the larder for some fun,
Round about the dishes creep,
Taking into each a peep,
To choose the daintiest that's there,
Spoiling things you do not care.

27 June • The Mouse, the Frog and the Little Red Hen • Anon.

This rhyme is a fable. Hailing from America, it tries to teach children the importance of initiative and hard work. Walt Disney adapted it as a cartoon short called *The Wise Little Hen* (1934), which is noteworthy as Donald Duck's first onscreen appearance – he is one of the lazy animals refusing to help bake the bread.

Once a Mouse, a Frog and a Little Red Hen
Together kept a house;
The Frog was the laziest of frogs,
And lazier still was the Mouse.

The work all fell on the Little Red Hen,
Who had to get the wood,
And build the fires, and scrub, and cook,
And sometimes hunt the food.

One day, as she went scratching round,
She found a bag of rye;
Said she, 'Now who will make some bread?'
Said the lazy Mouse, 'Not I.'

'Nor I,' croaked the Frog as he drowsed in the shade,
Red Hen made no reply,
But flew around with bowl and spoon,
And mixed and stirred the rye.

'Who'll make the fire to bake the bread?'
Said the Mouse again, 'Not I,'
And, scarcely opening his sleepy eyes,
Frog made the same reply.

The Little Red Hen said never a word,
But a roaring fire she made;
And while the bread was baking brown,
'Who'll set the table?' she said.

'Not I,' said the sleepy Frog with a yawn;
'Nor I,' said the Mouse again.
So the table she set and the bread put on,
'Who'll eat this bread?' said the Hen.

'I will!' cried the Frog. 'And I!' squeaked the Mouse,
As they near the table drew:
'Oh, no, you won't!' said the Little Red Hen,
And away with the loaf she flew.

28 June • The Three Little Kittens • Anon.

Cats and kittens are other animals that make popular subjects for nursery rhymes. This one has been controversially attributed to Eliza Lee Follen (1787–1860). Although she was the first person to print the rhyme in 1853, she described the verses as 'traditional', so we can take her lead and remove her name as the author.

The three little kittens, they lost their mittens,
And they began to cry,
'Oh, mother dear, we sadly fear,
That we have lost our mittens.'
'What! Lost your mittens, you naughty kittens!
Then you shall have no pie.'
'Meow, meow, meow.'
'Then you shall have no pie.'

The three little kittens, they found their mittens,
And they began to cry,
'Oh, mother dear, see here, see here,
For we have found our mittens.'
'Put on your mittens, you silly kittens,
And you shall have some pie.'
'Purr, purr, purr,
Oh, let us have some pie.'

The three little kittens put on their mittens,
And soon ate up the pie,
'Oh, mother dear, we greatly fear,
That we have soiled our mittens.'

'What, soiled your mittens, you naughty kittens!'
Then they began to sigh,
'Meow, meow, meow,'
Then they began to sigh.

The three little kittens, they washed their mittens,
And hung them out to dry,
'Oh, mother dear, do you not hear,
That we have washed our mittens?'
'What, washed your mittens, then you're good kittens,
But I smell a rat close by.'
'Meow, meow, meow,
We smell a rat close by.'

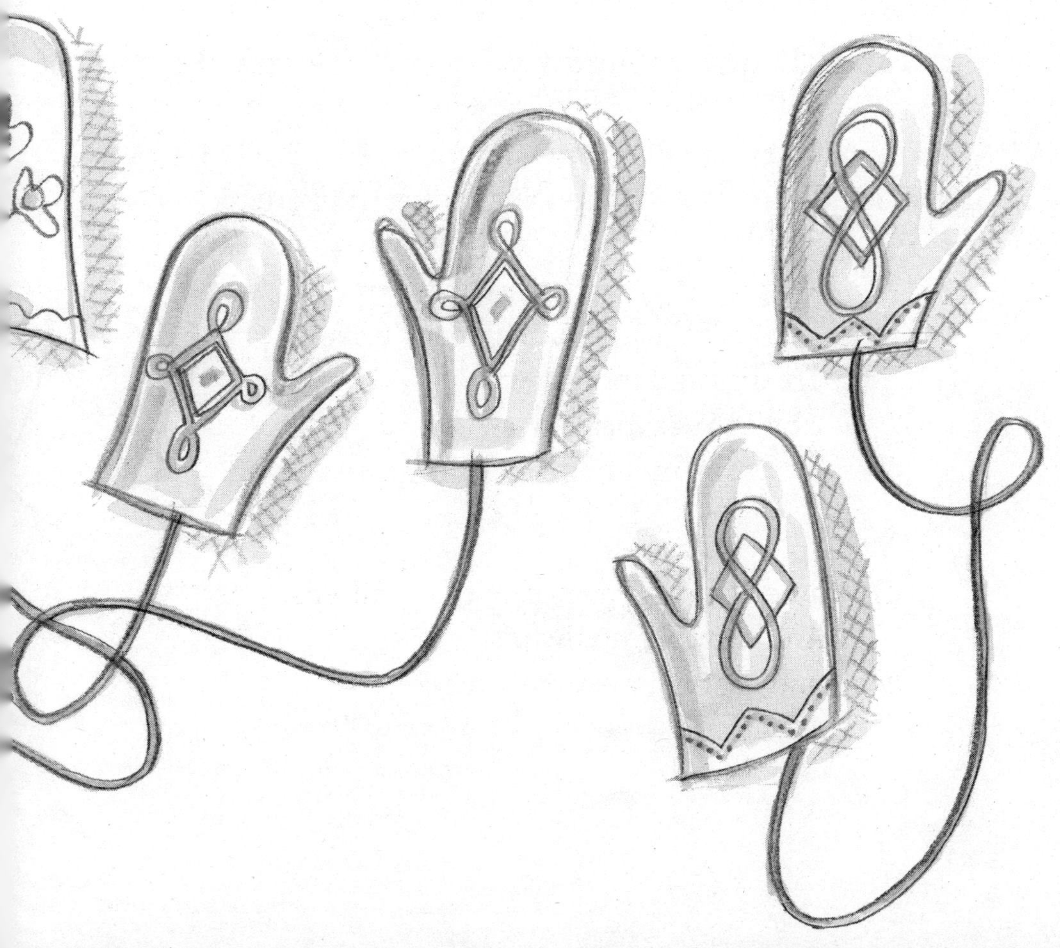

29 June • The Cat Sat Asleep by the Side of the Fire • Anon.

This feline rhyme dates back to at least 1707, and describes a scene with all the ingredients of a viral YouTube video – cats, dancing and embarrassing snores.

The cat sat asleep by the side of the fire,
  The mistress snored loud as a pig;
Jack took up his fiddle by Jenny's desire,
  And struck up a bit of a jig.

30 June • Diggory Diggory Delvet! • Beatrix Potter

Finally, to end this run of animal rhymes, here is a limerick about a mole, by *Peter Rabbit* author Beatrix Potter.

Diggory Diggory Delvet!
    A little old man in black velvet;
He digs and he delves –
You can see for yourselves
    The mounds dug by Diggory Delvet.

Weather Lore, Travel, Classics

1 July • Oh, Mister Sun • Anon.

July is a month for sunshine — but as these first few rhymes make clear, sunny weather is not guaranteed.

Oh, Mister Sun, Sun, Mister Golden Sun,
Please shine down on me.

Oh, Mister Sun, Sun, Mister Golden Sun,
Hiding behind a tree;
These little children are asking you
Please come out so we can play with you.

Oh, Mister Sun, Sun, Mister Golden Sun,
Please shine down on me.

2 July • A Sunshiny Shower • Anon.

How often do you think this weather lore is true?

A sunshiny shower
Won't last half-an-hour.

Rain before seven,
Fine by eleven.

3 July • Red Sky at Night • Anon.

This weather warning has been around for a very long time; it can even be found in the Bible (Matthew 16:2-3).

Red sky at night,
Shepherd's delight;
Red sky in the morning,
Shepherd's warning.

4 July • When the Sand Doth Feed the Clay • Anon.

The sand is said to feed the clay after a wet summer, and the clay feeds the sand after a dry summer. In England, a dry summer is good for the harvest, but the reverse is true for Southern Europe.

When the sand doth feed the clay,
England woe and well-a-day!
But when the clay doth feed the sand,
Then it is well with Angle-land.

5 July • Three Children Sliding on the Ice • Anon.

This has been attributed both to John Gay (1685–1732) and Oliver Goldsmith (1728–1774). However, as it was printed back in 1662 before either of them were born, we can safely assume these attributions are as nonsensical as the rhyme itself.

Three children sliding on the ice
 Upon a summer's day,
As it fell out, they all fell in,
 The rest they ran away.

Oh, had these children been at school,
 Or sliding on dry ground,
Ten thousand pounds to one penny
 They had not then been drowned.

Ye parents who have children dear,
 And eke ye that have none,
If you would keep them safe abroad,
 Pray keep them safe at home.

6 July • From Wibbleton to Wobbleton • Anon.

This lap song is designed to be sung in motion. Bounce your child on your lap through your singing of the song, but when you sing 'for Wibbleton', bounce the child on your left knee, while on 'for Wobbleton', bounce the child on your right knee.

From Wibbleton to Wobbleton is fifteen miles.
From Wobbleton to Wibbleton is fifteen miles.
From Wibbleton to Wobbleton, from Wobbleton to Wibbleton,
From Wibbleton to Wobbleton is fifteen miles.

7 July • Puff the Magic Dragon • Peter Yarrow and Leonard Lipton

This song was released in 1963 by the American folk group Peter, Paul and Mary. Tech pioneer Elon Musk named the SpaceX Dragon spacecraft after Puff!

Puff, the magic dragon,
Lived by the sea
And frolicked in the autumn mist
In a land called Honalee.
Little Jackie Paper
Loved that rascal Puff
And brought him strings and sealing wax
And other fancy stuff.

Oh, Puff, the magic dragon
Lived by the sea
And frolicked in the autumn mist
In a land called Honalee.

Together they would travel
On a boat with billowed sail
Jackie kept a look-out
Perched on Puff's gigantic tail.
Noble kings and princes
Would bow whene'er they came,
Pirate ships would lower their flags
When Puff roared out his name.

Oh, Puff, the magic dragon
Lived by the sea
And frolicked in the autumn mist
In a land called Honalee.

A dragon lives forever
But not so, little boys.
Painted wings and giants' rings
Make way for other toys.
One grey night it happened,
Jackie Paper came no more,
And Puff, that mighty dragon,
He ceased his fearless roar.

His head was bent in sorrow
Green scales fell like rain,
Puff no longer went to play
Along the cherry lane.
Without his lifelong friend
Puff could not be brave.
So Puff, that mighty dragon,
Sadly slipped into his cave.

Oh, Puff, the magic dragon
Lived by the sea
And frolicked in the autumn mist
In a land called Honalee.
Puff, the magic dragon
Lived by the sea
And frolicked in the autumn mist
In a land called Honalee.

8 July • Zoom, Zoom, Zoom • Anon.

This space-travel nursery rhyme is usually recited to children by a grown-up who then gently throws them into the air on 'Blast off'. Grown-ups – remember to catch them on touch down!

Zoom, zoom, zoom,
We're going to the moon.
Zoom, zoom, zoom,
We're going to the moon.
If you want to take a trip,
Climb aboard my rocket ship.
Zoom, zoom, zoom,
We're going to the moon,
5, 4, 3, 2, 1,
Blast off!

9 July • Row, Row, Row Your Boat • Anon.

Moving from rocket ships to boats, here is another very well-known nursery rhyme, to which children often add irreverent endings such as 'Ha-ha, fooled you! / I'm a submarine'.

Row, row, row your boat,
Gently down the stream,
Merrily, merrily, merrily, merrily,
Life is but a dream.

Row, row, row your boat,
Gently down the stream,
If you see a crocodile,
Don't forget to scream!

10 July • I've Never Sailed the Amazon • Rudyard Kipling

The Jungle Book author Rudyard Kipling (1865–1936) included these verses at the end of 'The Beginning of the Armadillos', one of his *Just So Stories* (1902). Despite his pessimistic belief that he 'never will' get to make this journey, twenty-five years after writing it, in the spring of 1927, he and his wife actually did fulfil his dream of travelling to Brazil via a ship from Southampton!

I've never sailed the Amazon,
    I've never reached Brazil;
But the *Don* and *Magdalena*,
    They can go there when they will!

        Yes, weekly from Southampton,
        Great steamers, white and gold,
        Go rolling down to Rio
        (Roll down – roll down to Rio!).
        And I'd like to roll to Rio
        Some day before I'm old!

I've never seen a Jaguar,
    Nor yet an Armadill-
O dilloing in his armour,
    And I s'pose I never will,

        Unless I go to Rio
        These wonders to behold –
        Roll down – roll down to Rio –
        Roll really down to Rio!
        Oh, I'd love to roll to Rio
        Some day before I'm old!

11 July • A Peanut Sat on a Railroad Track • Anon.

Let's leave the sea and join the railway with a tragicomical rhyme.

A peanut sat on a railroad track,
His heart was all a-flutter.
The five-fifteen came rushing by –
Toot toot! Peanut butter!

12 July • Down at the Station • Anon.

The 'puffer trains' in this rhyme are old-fashioned steam-engine trains, first invented in the UK in the early nineteenth century.

Down at the station, early in the morning,
See the little puffer trains, all in a row.
Here comes the driver to start up the engine,
Puff! Puff! Peep! Peep! Off we go!
Puff! Puff! Peep! Peep! Off we go!
Puff! Puff! Peep! Peep! Off we go!

Down at the station, early in the morning,
See the little puffer trains, all in a row.
Here comes the driver to start up the engine,
Chuff! Chuff! Toot! Toot! Off we go!
Chuff! Chuff! Toot! Toot! Off we go!
Chuff! Chuff! Toot! Toot! Off we go!

Down at the station, early in the morning,
See the little puffer trains, all in a row.
Here comes the driver to start up the engine,
Clickety clack! Clickety clack! Off we go!
Clickety clack! Clickety clack! Off we go!
Clickety clack! Clickety clack! Off we go!

13 July • Toy Train • Rod Campbell

Here is another sweet rhyme by Scottish author Rod Campbell where travel takes place in the nursery.

> Clackety clack,
> Clackety clack,
> The toy train's chugging
> Round the track.
>
> Where are the toys going today?
> Over the hills and far away;
> To strange lands across the sea,
> And home again in time for tea!

14 July • We're Goin' on a Bear Hunt • Anon.

This traditional American call-and-response camp song was adapted into the wildly successful Michael Rosen book *We're Going on a Bear Hunt* in 1989. More recently, during the Covid-19 pandemic, people across the world put stuffed bears in their windows so that children could do 'bear hunts' during their walks.

We're goin' on a bear hunt
(We're goin' on a bear hunt)
We're going to catch a big one
(We're going to catch a big one)
I'm not scared
(I'm not scared)
What a beautiful day!
(What a beautiful day!)

Uh-uh!
Grass!
Long wavy grass.
We can't go over it.
We can't go under it.
Oh no!
We've got to go through it!
Swishy swashy! Swishy swashy!
    Swishy swashy!

We're goin' on a bear hunt
(We're goin' on a bear hunt)
We're going to catch a big one
(We're going to catch a big one)
I'm not scared
(I'm not scared)
What a beautiful day!
(What a beautiful day!)

Uh-uh!
A river!
A deep cold river.
We can't go over it.
We can't go under it.
Oh no!
We've got to go through it!
Splash splosh! Splash splosh! Splash splosh!

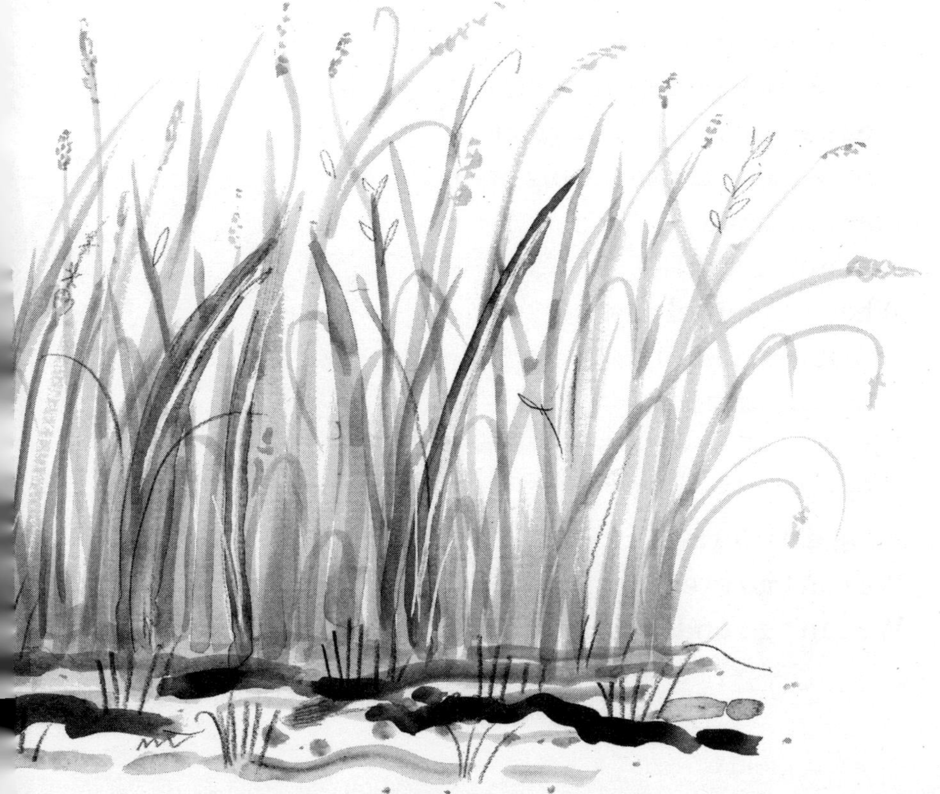

We're goin' on a bear hunt
(We're goin' on a bear hunt)
We're going to catch a big one
(We're going to catch a big one)
I'm not scared
(I'm not scared)
What a beautiful day!
(What a beautiful day!)

Uh-uh!
Mud!
Thick oozy mud.
We can't go over it,
We can't go under it.
Oh no!
We've got to go through it!
Squelch squerch! Squelch squerch! Squelch squerch!

We're goin' on a bear hunt
(We're goin' on a bear hunt)
We're going to catch a big one
(We're going to catch a big one)
I'm not scared
(I'm not scared)
What a beautiful day!
(What a beautiful day!)

Uh-uh!
A forest!
A big dark forest.
We can't go over it.
We can't go under it.

Oh no!
We've got to go through it!
Stumble trip! Stumble trip! Stumble trip!

We're goin' on a bear hunt
(We're goin' on a bear hunt)
We're going to catch a big one
(We're going to catch a big one)
I'm not scared
(I'm not scared)
What a beautiful day!
(What a beautiful day!)

Uh-uh!
A snowstorm!
A swirling whirling snowstorm.
We can't go over it.
We can't go under it.
Oh no!
We've got to go through it!
Hooo wooo! Hooo wooo! Hooo wooo!

We're goin' on a bear hunt
(We're goin' on a bear hunt)
We're going to catch a big one
(We're going to catch a big one)
I'm not scared
(I'm not scared)
What a beautiful day!
(What a beautiful day!)

Uh-uh!
A cave!
A narrow gloomy cave.
We can't go over it.
We can't go under it.
We've got to go through it!
Tiptoe! Tiptoe! Tiptoe!
WHAT'S THAT?
One shiny wet nose!
Two big furry ears!
Two big goggly eyes!
IT'S A BEAR!

Quick!
Back through the cave!
Tiptoe! Tiptoe! Tiptoe!
Back through the snowstorm!
Hoooo woooo! Hoooo woooo! Hoooo woooo!
Back through the forest!
Stumble trip! Stumble trip! Stumble trip!
Back through the mud!
Squelch squerch! Squelch squerch! Squelch squerch!
Back through the river!
Splash splosh! Splash splosh! Splash splosh!
Back through the grass!
Swishy swashy! Swishy swashy! Swishy swashy!
Get to our front door.
Open the door.
Up the stairs
Oh no!

15 July • How Many Miles to Babylon? • Anon.

In Elizabethan times, 'Can I get there by candle-light?' was a common saying. This has been largely replaced by 'Can I get there by Uber?'

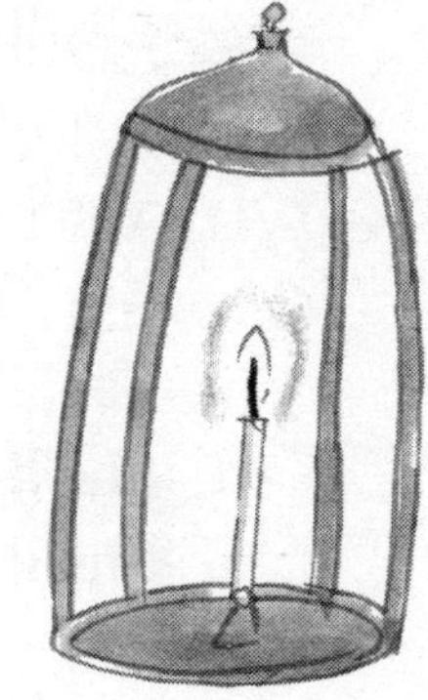

'How many miles to Babylon?'
'Threescore miles and ten.'
'Can I get there by candle-light?'
'Yes and back again!
If your heels are nimble and light,
You may get there by candle-light.'

16 July • She'll Be Comin' Round the Mountain • Anon.

This nursery rhyme originated as an African American spiritual ('When the Chariot Comes'), which was turned into the present song by mountaineers, and spread across to railroad workers in the late nineteenth century. Its twentieth-century life has been eventful, to say the least. To the same tune, there is a Scottish children's song ('Ye Cannae Shove Yer Granny Off a Bus') and a University of Cambridge sports chant levelled against the teams of St John's College ('We would rather be at Oxford than St John's').

She'll be comin' round the mountain,
    When she comes.
She'll be comin' round the mountain,
    When she comes.

She'll be comin' round the mountain,
She'll be comin' round the mountain,
She'll be comin' round the mountain,
    When she comes.

She'll be drivin' six white horses,
    When she comes.
She'll be drivin' six white horses,
    When she comes.
She'll be drivin' six white horses,
She'll be drivin' six white horses,
She'll be drivin' six white horses,
    When she comes.

Oh we'll all go to meet her,
    When she comes.
Oh we'll all go to meet her,
    When she comes.
We will kill the old red rooster,
We will kill the old red rooster,
And we'll all have chicken and dumplin',
    When she comes.

17 July • The Bear Went Over the Mountain • Anon.

This bear is on the hunt for . . . something. Or maybe he just likes to travel and take in the views. In any case, this popular campfire song is sung to the tune of 'For He's a Jolly Good Fellow', and can incorporate all kinds of movement. With each repetition of the verse, you might want to change your interpretation of walking over the mountain. Or, if you prefer, have your fingers represent the action! This is the perfect tune to allow your child their own imaginative experience. What did the bear see over the mountain?

Oh, the bear went over the mountain,
The bear went over the mountain,
The bear went over the mountain,
To see what he could see.

But all that he could see,
But all that he could see,
Was the other side of the mountain,
The other side of the mountain,
The other side of the mountain,
Was all that he could see.

So he went back over the mountain,
He went back over the mountain,
He went back over the mountain,
To see what he could see.

But all that he could see,
But all that he could see,
Was the other side of the mountain,

The other side of the mountain,
The other side of the mountain,
Was all that he could see.
All that he could see!

18 July • It's a Long Way to Tipperary • Traditional

It's 350 miles from London to Tipperary where the speaker of this music-hall song has left his heart. The authorship is disputed but a recording made close to the outbreak of the First World War propelled the song to popularity as it was sung by soldiers marching off to war. As you enter the Irish town of Tipperary today, there's a sign in homage to the song that says: *You've Come a Long Way*.

Up to mighty London
Came an Irishman one day.
As the streets are paved with gold
Sure, everyone was gay,
Singing songs of Piccadilly,
Strand and Leicester Square,
Till Paddy got excited,
Then he shouted to them there.

It's a long way to Tipperary,
It's a long way to go.
It's a long way to Tipperary,
To the sweetest girl I know!
Goodbye, Piccadilly,
Farewell, Leicester Square!
It's a long, long way to Tipperary,
But my heart's right there.

Paddy wrote a letter
To his Irish Molly-O,
Saying, 'Should you not receive it,
Write and let me know!
If I make mistakes in spelling,
Molly, dear,' said he,
'Remember, it's the pen that's bad,
Don't lay the blame on *me*!'

It's a long way to Tipperary,
It's a long way to go.
It's a long way to Tipperary,
To the sweetest girl I know!
Goodbye, Piccadilly,
Farewell, Leicester Square!
It's a long, long way to Tipperary,
But my heart's right there.

Molly wrote a neat reply
To Irish Paddy-O,
Saying, 'Mike Maloney
Wants to marry me, and so
Leave The Strand and Piccadilly
Or you'll be to blame,
For love has fairly drove me silly:
Hoping you're the same!'

It's a long way to Tipperary,
It's a long way to go.
It's a long way to Tipperary,
To the sweetest girl I know!
Goodbye, Piccadilly,
Farewell, Leicester Square!
It's a long long way to Tipperary,
But my heart's right there.

19 July • Pack Up Your Troubles in Your Old Kit-Bag • George Henry Powell

Written by Welshman George Henry Powell (1880–1951), these lyrics were also adopted by soldiers as a marching song in the First World War. Interestingly, Powell was a pacifist and conscientious objector.

Pack up your troubles in your old kit-bag
And smile, smile, smile,
Don't let your joy and laughter hear the snag,
Smile, boys, that's the style.
What's the use of worrying?
It never was worthwhile
So pack up your troubles in your old kit-bag
And smile, smile, smile.

20 July • Little Miss Muffet • Anon.

Now we move on to classic nursery rhymes, which have been circulating for generations and many of whose subjects are full of mystery. However, Miss Muffet of today's rhyme is believed to have been a real person – the daughter of Thomas Muffet, the sixteenth-century entomologist (insect specialist). Most of these rhymes have travelled across time and even across the globe; in Jamaica, there is a patois variant which reads: 'Lickle Miss Julie / Kotch pon ar stoolie / An nyam wan ripe Bombay / Den bredda Anancy / Come frighten de pickney / An tief de ripe mango away.' ('Anancy' is based on the trickster god Anansi, in Akan folklore.)

Little Miss Muffet
Sat on a tuffet,
Eating her curds and whey;
Along came a spider,
Who sat down beside her,
And frightened Miss Muffet away.

21 July • Lucy Locket Lost her Pocket • Anon.

The name Lucy Lockit in John Gay's *The Beggar's Opera* (1728) may have either inspired or been inspired by the Lucy of this rhyme. A pocket was a pouch or purse.

Lucy Locket lost her pocket
Kitty Fisher found it;
There was not a penny in it,
But a ribbon round it.

22 July • Oh Where, Oh Where Has my Little Dog Gone? • Septimus Winner

The original lyrics of this song were written in 1864 by the American entertainer Septimus Winner (1827–1905), who set it to the tune of an old German folk song called 'In Lauterbach hab' ich mein' Strumpf verlor'n' (in which it is a stocking, not a dog, that has gone missing).

Oh where, oh where has my little dog gone?
  Oh where, oh where can he be?
With his ears cut short and his tail cut long,
  Oh where, oh where can he be?
Oh where, oh where has my little dog gone?
  Oh where, oh where can he be?

23 July • Dance to Your Daddy • Anon.

Fathers can sing this traditional Scottish song to their children. (In the second verse, Daddy promises a little coat, a pair of trousers, a spinning-top and a doll.)

Dance to your daddy,
My bonnie laddie,
Dance to your daddy, my bonnie lamb!
And you'll get a fishie
In a little dishie,
You'll get a fishie, when the boat comes home.

Dance to your daddy,
My bonnie laddie,
Dance to your daddy, my bonnie lamb!
And you'll get a coatie,
And a pair of breekies,
You'll get a whippie and a soople tam.

24 July • This is the House that Jack Built • Anon.

This cumulative verse, another in the ever-expanding tradition, begins a run of nursery rhymes about people called Jack – of which there are a surprising number! One of the reasons for this, aside from it being a fairly common name, is that in times of yore, 'Jack' was a nickname used to refer to anyone considered to be a rogue or a cheeky rascal – we all know a few!

This is the house that Jack built.

This is the malt
That lay in the house that Jack built.

This is the rat
That ate the malt
That lay in the house that Jack built.

This is the cat
That killed the rat
That ate the malt
That lay in the house that Jack built.

This is the dog
That worried the cat
That killed the rat
That ate the malt,
That lay in the house that Jack built.

This is the cow with the crumpled horn
That tossed the dog
That worried the cat
That killed the rat
That ate the malt
That lay in the house that Jack built.

This is the maiden all forlorn
That milked the cow with the crumpled horn
That tossed the dog
That worried the cat
That killed the rat
That ate the malt
That lay in the house that Jack built.

This is the man all tattered and torn
That kissed the maiden all forlorn
That milked the cow with the crumpled horn
That tossed the dog
That worried the cat
That killed the rat
That ate the malt
That lay in the house that Jack built.

This is the priest all shaven and shorn
That married the man all tattered and torn
That kissed the maiden all forlorn
That milked the cow with the crumpled horn
That tossed the dog
That worried the cat
That killed the rat
That ate the malt
That lay in the house that Jack built.

This is the cock that crowed in the morn
That waked the priest all shaven and shorn
That married the man all tattered and torn
That kissed the maiden all forlorn
That milked the cow with the crumpled horn

That tossed the dog
That worried the cat
That killed the rat
That ate the malt
That lay in the house that Jack built.

This is the farmer sowing his corn
That kept the cock that crowed in the morn
That waked the priest all shaven and shorn
That married the man all tattered and torn
That kissed the maiden all forlorn
That milked the cow with the crumpled horn
That tossed the dog
That worried the cat
That killed the rat
That ate the malt
That lay in the house that Jack built.

25 July • Jack Sprat Could Eat No Fat • Anon.

In the 1500s and 1600s, 'Jack Sprat' was a term for a man of unusually short stature. An early version of this rhyme comes from John Clarke's 1639 proverb collection: 'Jack will eat no fat, and Jill doth love no leane / Yet betwixt them both they lick the dishes cleane.' It is the rhyming equivalent of the saying that 'opposites attract'.

Jack Sprat could eat no fat,
    His wife could eat no lean,
And so between them both, you see,
    They licked the platter clean.

26 July • Jack and Jill Went up the Hill • Anon.

The question of why Jack and Jill would head uphill for water has mystified commentators, who often assume some ancient significance must be attached to it. There are multiple variants of the nursery rhyme but the first verse has not varied and its rhyming of 'water' with 'after' suggests it has been around since the early seventeenth century when the pronunciation would have been 'wahter' and 'ahter'.

Jack and Jill went up the hill
  To fetch a pail of water;
Jack fell down and broke his crown,
  And Jill came tumbling after.

Up Jack got, and home did trot,
  As fast as he could caper,
Went to bed to mend his head
  With vinegar and brown paper.

27 July • Jack Be Nimble • Anon.

In England, the game of candle-leaping was historically associated with this well- known rhyme. A lit candle would be placed on the floor, and players would take turns jumping over it. If you managed to jump over the candlestick without blowing out the candle, good luck was promised. Do not try this at home.

Jack be nimble,
Jack be quick,
Jack jump over
The candlestick.

28 July • Doctor Foster went to Glo'ster • Anon.

This nursery rhyme is difficult to date due to a lack of print sources, but the rhyming of 'puddle' and 'middle' suggests it is very old (when the word 'piddle' meant a small body of rainwater). It could be about Doctor Faustus, the alchemist hero of an Elizabethan play by Christopher Marlowe, who, in a comic scene, sells someone a horse and tells him not to ride it into water. When the customer ignores him, and rides into water, the horse melts into hay and its rider is left struggling.

Doctor Foster went to Glo'ster
In a shower of rain;
He stepped in a puddle, right up to his middle,
And never went there again.

29 July • Robert Barnes, Fellow Fine • Anon.

This nursery rhyme might still be recited in the forges of working blacksmiths, but it has also evolved to be a rhyme used whilst trying to fit children's shoes on their reluctant feet. It is thought to have originated in Northern England, but there is a similar rhyme found in old Scottish collections: 'John Smith, fallow fine / Can you shoe this horse o' mine? / Aye, indeed, and that I can, / As well as ony man! / There's a nail upon the tae, / To make the powny speel the brae; / There's a nail and there's a brod / – a horse weel shod.'

'Robert Barnes, fellow fine,
Can you shoe this horse of mine?'
'Yes, good sir, that I can,
As well as any other man;
Here's a nail, and there's a prod,
And now, good sir, your horse is shod.'

30 July • Horsie, Horsie, Don't You Stop • Anon.

Horses come in for attention again in this classic rhyme, often recited on the back of a hobby horse.

Horsie, horsie, don't you stop,
Just let your feet go clippety clop,
Your tail goes swish and the wheels go round,
Giddy-up, we're homeward bound.

Horsie, horsie, on your way,
We've done this journey many a day,
Your tail goes swish and the wheels go round,
Giddy-up, we're homeward bound.

31 July • There Was a Crooked Man, and He Walked a Crooked Mile • Anon

To end this run of classic nursery rhymes, here is one that tells of perfect – albeit crooked – harmony.

There was a crooked man, and he walked a crooked mile,
He found a crooked sixpence against a crooked stile;
He bought a crooked cat, which caught a crooked mouse,
And they all lived together in a little crooked house.

August

Sea, Rivers, Outdoors

1 August • She Sells Seashells by the Seashore • Anon.

For August, we begin with a run of rhymes about the sea, starting with this tongue-twister. It's widely claimed to be about the fossil collector Mary Anning (1799–1847). Some even say she wrote it herself.

> She sells seashells by the seashore.
> The shells that she sells are seashells, I'm sure.
> So if she sells seashells by the seashore,
> The shells that she sells are seashells for sure.

2 August • Bobby Shaftoe's Gone to Sea • Anon.

This traditional Scottish rhyme takes us from the beach to the sea. It was used by the supporters of the English Tory MP Robert Shaftoe (1732–1797) as a campaign song when he successfully stood for Parliament in 1761.

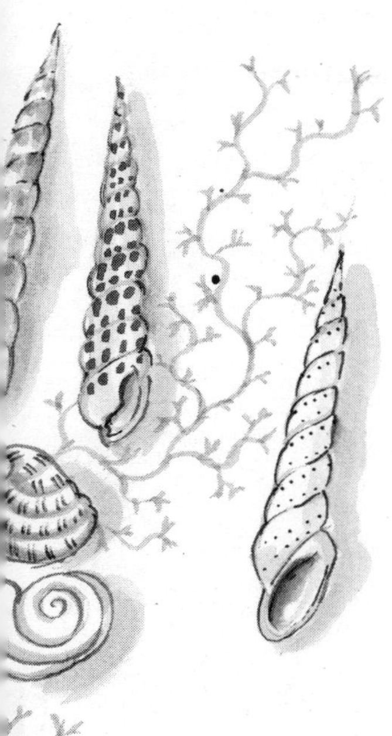

Bobby Shaftoe's gone to sea,
    Silver buckles at his knee;
He'll come back and marry me,
    Bonny Bobby Shaftoe.

Bobby Shaftoe's bright and fair,
    Combing down his yellow hair,
He's my love for evermore
    Bonny Bobby Shaftoe.

Bobby Shaftoe's looking out
    All his ribbons flew about
All the ladies gave a shout
    Hey for Bobby Shaftoe!

3 August • My Bonnie Lies Over the Ocean • Anon.

This is another Scottish folk song, which emerged during the MP Bobby Shaftoe's lifetime – sung by supporters of Bonnie Prince Charlie (1720–1788), whose claim to the British throne ended in defeat and exile in 1746. It is perhaps the most versatile rhyme in the book, and has been covered by many different musicians. Jazz icon Ella Fitzgerald recorded it, accompanied by a calypso band, The Beatles did a rock'n'roll rendition, and Carly Simon has turned it into a lullaby medley with 'Hush, Little Baby'.

My Bonnie lies over the ocean
My Bonnie lies over the sea
My Bonnie lies over the ocean
Oh, bring back my Bonnie to me.

Bring back, bring back
Oh, bring back my Bonnie to me, to me
Bring back, bring back
Oh, bring back my Bonnie to me.

Oh blow ye winds over the ocean
Oh blow ye winds over the sea
Oh blow ye winds over the ocean
And bring back my Bonnie to me.

Bring back, bring back
Oh, bring back my Bonnie to me, to me
Bring back, bring back
Oh, bring back my Bonnie to me.

Last night as I lay on my pillow
Last night as I lay on my bed
Last night as I lay on my pillow
I dreamt that my Bonnie was dead.

Bring back, bring back
Oh, bring back my Bonnie to me, to me
Bring back, bring back
Oh, bring back my Bonnie to me.

The winds have blown over the ocean
The winds have blown over the sea
The winds have blown over the ocean
And brought back my Bonnie to me.

Bring back, bring back
Oh, bring back my Bonnie to me, to me
Bring back, bring back
Oh, bring back my Bonnie to me.

4 August • I Saw a Ship a-Sailing • Anon.

Scholars speculate that Sir Francis Drake (1540–1596), the Elizabethan explorer and sea captain, might be the subject of this old rhyme. After all, he did bring 'comfits' such as sugared apricots and grapes home from his travels, and the captain in the rhyme is a duck!

I saw a ship a-sailing,
  A-sailing on the sea;
And, oh! it was laden
  With pretty things for thee!

There were comfits in the cabin,
  And apples in the hold,
The sails were made of silk,
  And the masts were made of gold.

The four-and-twenty sailors
  That stood between the decks,
Were four-and-twenty white mice
  With chains around their necks.

The captain was a duck,
  With a packet on his back;
And when the ship began to move,
  The captain said, 'Quack! quack!'

5 August • A Sailor Went to Sea • Anon.

This rhyme about sailors is accompanied by actions. Traditionally a hand does an action for a wave at each repetition of ‘sea sea sea’, a salute for each ‘see see see’, a chopping movement against the other arm for ‘chop chop chop’ and a tap on the knee for ‘knee knee knee’.

A sailor went to sea sea sea
To see what he could see see see
But all that he could see see see
Was the bottom of the deep blue sea sea sea.

A sailor went to chop chop chop
To see what he could chop chop chop
But all that he could chop chop chop
Was the bottom of the deep blue chop chop chop.

A sailor went to knee knee knee
To see what he could knee knee knee
But all that he could knee knee knee
Was the bottom of the deep blue knee knee knee.

A sailor went to sea, chop, knee
To see what he could sea, chop, knee
But all that he could sea, chop, knee
Was the bottom of the deep blue sea, chop, knee.

6 August • I Had Three Sisters Across the Sea • Anon.

The way nursery rhymes survive through the oral tradition is demonstrated by the endurance of another baffling rhyme. The first record we have of this one is in a manuscript dating from 1440, then there is no document of it again for nearly 400 years, until it re-appeared in the book *Ancient Scottish Melodies* in 1838.

I had three sisters across the sea,
Peerie, weerie, winkum, do, re, me;
What handsome presents they all sent me,
Pinkum, quartum, Paradise lost them,
Peerie, weerie, winkum, do, re, me.

The first was a chicken without a bone,
Peerie, weerie, winkum, do, re, me;
The second was a cherry without a stone,
Pinkum, quartum, Paradise lost them,
Peerie, weerie, winkum, do, re, me.

The third was a blanket without a thread
Peerie, weerie, winkum, do, re, me;
The fourth was a book that couldn't be read,
Pinkum, quartum, Paradise lost them,
Peerie, weerie, winkum, do, re, me.

How could there be a chicken without a bone?
Peerie, weerie, winkum, do, re, me;
How could there be a cherry without a stone?
Pinkum, quartum, Paradise lost them,
Peerie, weerie, winkum, do, re, me.

How could there be a blanket without a thread?
    Peerie, weerie, winkum, do, re, me;
How could there be a book that couldn't be read?
    Pinkum, quartum, Paradise lost them,
        Peerie, weerie, winkum, do, re, me.

The chicken in the egg without a bone,
    Peerie, weerie, winkum, do, re, me;
The cherry in the blossom without a stone,
    Pinkum, quartum, Paradise lost them,
        Peerie, weerie, winkum, do, re, me.

The blanket in the fleece without a thread,
    Peerie, weerie, winkum, do, re, me;
The book in the press that couldn't be read,
    Pinkum, quartum, Paradise lost them,
        Peerie, weerie, winkum, do, re, me.

7 August • I am a Claddagh Boatman Bold • Anon.

This Irish 'boatman's ditty' is set in Claddagh – a former fishing village just outside the city walls of Galway, where the River Corrib meets Galway Bay.

I am a Claddagh boatman bold,
  And humble is my calling,
From morn to night, from dark to light,
  In Galway Bay I'm trawling;
I care not for the great man's from,
  I ask not for his pity;
My wants are few, my heart is true,
  I sing a boatman's ditty.

I have a fair and gentle wife,
  Her name is Eily Holway;
With many a wile, and joke, and smile,
  I won the pride of Galway.
For twenty years, 'mid hopes and fears,
  With her I've faithful tarried;
Her heart to-night is young and light
  As when we first were married.

I have a son, a gallant boy,
  Unstained by spot or speckle;
He pulls and hauls, and mends the trawls,
  And minds the other tackle.
His mother says, the boy, like me,
  Loves truth, and hates all blarney.
The neighbours swear, in Galway Bay
  There's not the like of Barney.

Thank God, I have another child,
Like Eily, lithe and slender;
She clasps my knee, and kisses me
With love so true and tender.
Though oft will rage the howling blast
Upon the angry water,
I ne'er complain of wind or rain,
For I think of my little daughter.

When Sunday brings the hours of rest,
That sweet reward of labours,
We cross the fields to early Mass,
And walk home with our neighbours.
O, would the rest of Erin's sons
Were but like us united;
To swear I'm loath, but, by my oath,
Her name should not be slighted.

8 August • What Shall We Do with the Drunken Sailor? • Anon.

It's time for a well-known pirate song. Sea shanties were used by merchant sailors to keep the crew in time with tasks – and this one is known to have been sung on ships at least as early as 1830.

> What shall we do with the drunken sailor,
> What shall we do with the drunken sailor,
> What shall we do with the drunken sailor,
>   Ear-lie in the morning?
> Hoo-ray and up she rises,
> Hoo-ray and up she rises,
> Hoo-ray and up she rises,
>   Ear-lie in the morning.

9 August • The Wellerman • Anon.

A nineteenth-century New Zealand sea shanty became a surprise hit on TikTok in the summer of 2021. Nathan Evans, a Scottish postman, uploaded his version on the platform, which then triggered a viral craze totalling tens of millions of views. The song refers to the supply ships of the brothers Edward, George and Joseph Weller, who provided 'sugar and tea and rum' to New Zealand whalers.

There once was a ship that put to sea
And the name of that ship was the *Billy o' Tea*
The winds blew hard, her bow dipped down
  Blow, me bully boys, blow.

Soon may the Wellerman come
To bring us sugar and tea and rum
One day, when the tonguin' is done
  We'll take our leave and go.

She had not been two weeks from shore
When down on her a right whale bore
The captain called all hands and swore
  He'd take that whale in tow.

Soon may the Wellerman come
To bring us sugar and tea and rum
One day, when the tonguin' is done
  We'll take our leave and go.

Before the boat had hit the water
The whale's tail came up and caught her
All hands to the side, harpooned and fought her
    When she dived down below.

Soon may the Wellerman come
To bring us sugar and tea and rum
One day, when the tonguin' is done
    We'll take our leave and go.

No line was cut, no whale was freed
The Captain's mind was not on greed
But he belonged to the whaleman's creed
    She took that ship in tow.

Soon may the Wellerman come
To bring us sugar and tea and rum
One day, when the tonguin' is done
    We'll take our leave and go.

For forty days, or even more
The line went slack, then tight once more
All boats were lost, there were only four
  But still that whale did go.

Soon may the Wellerman come
To bring us sugar and tea and rum
One day, when the tonguin' is done
  We'll take our leave and go.

As far as I've heard, the fight's still on,
The line's not cut and the whale's not gone
The Wellerman makes his a regular call
  To encourage the Captain, crew, and all.

Soon may the Wellerman come
To bring us sugar and tea and rum
One day, when the tonguin' is done
  We'll take our leave and go.

10 August • When I Was ONE I Sucked my Thumb • Anon.

There are many different first lines of this pirate song including, 'When I was ONE I'd just begun', 'When I was ONE I played my drum', and even 'When I was ONE I swallowed a bun' – so feel free to invent your own!

When I was ONE I sucked my thumb,
The day I went to sea.
I jumped aboard a pirate ship,
And the captain said to me –
We're going this way, that way,
Forwards and backwards,
Over the Irish Sea,
We're going this way, that way,
Forwards and backwards,
That's the life for me!

When I was TWO I buckled my shoe,
The day I went to sea.
I jumped aboard a pirate ship,
And the captain said to me –
We're going this way, that way,
Forwards and backwards,
Over the Irish Sea,
We're going this way, that way,
Forwards and backwards,
That's the life for me!

When I was THREE I bashed my knee,
The day I went to sea.
I jumped aboard a pirate ship,
And the captain said to me –
We're going this way, that way,
Forwards and backwards,
Over the Irish Sea,
We're going this way, that way,
Forwards and backwards,
That's the life for me!

When I was FOUR I knocked on the door,
The day I went to sea.
I jumped aboard a pirate ship,
And the captain said to me –
We're going this way, that way,
Forwards and backwards,
Over the Irish Sea,
We're going this way, that way,
Forwards and backwards,
That's the life for me!

When I was FIVE I learnt to dive,
The day I went to sea.
I jumped aboard a pirate ship,
And the captain said to me –
We're going this way, that way,
Forwards and backwards,
Over the Irish Sea,
We're going this way, that way,
Forwards and backwards,
That's the life for me!

11 August • Five Old Fishermen • Anon.

The junk found in modern waterways is the more inauspicious theme of this comic rhyme. A 'tiddler' is a small fish, and a 'perambulator' is the proper name for a baby's pram.

Five old fishermen
Sitting on a bridge
One caught a tiddler
One caught a fridge.
One caught a tadpole
One caught an eel
And the fifth one caught
A perambulator wheel.

12 August • On the Muddy Bank of the Zambezi • Uzo Unobagha

This is another rhyme by contemporary Nigerian author Uzo Unobagha. The Zambezi is Africa's longest east-flowing river, stretching from Zambia to Mozambique.

On the muddy bank of the Zambezi,
Danced the Queen of the Fish;
She danced until she was dizzy
And fell right into my dish.

13 August • When Fishes Set Umbrellas Up • Christina Rossetti

Christina Rossetti gives us this sweet quatrain for the nursery.

When fishes set umbrellas up
    If the rain-drops run,
Lizards will want their parasols
    To shade them from the sun.

14 August • Baby Shark • Anon.

Originally an American campfire song, a simplified (and somewhat sanitized!) version of this nursery rhyme was explosively successful when Pinkfong recorded and released it on YouTube, with ten billion views and counting!

Baby shark, doo doo doo doo doo
Baby shark, doo doo doo doo doo
Baby shark, doo doo doo doo doo
Baby shark!

Mama shark, doo doo doo doo doo
Mama shark, doo doo doo doo doo
Mama shark, doo doo doo doo doo
Mama shark!

Papa shark, doo doo doo doo doo
Papa shark, doo doo doo doo doo
Papa shark, doo doo doo doo doo
Papa shark!

Grandma shark, doo doo doo doo doo
Grandma shark, doo doo doo doo doo
Grandma shark, doo doo doo doo doo
Grandma shark!

Surfer dude, doo doo doo doo doo
Surfer dude, doo doo doo doo doo
Surfer dude, doo doo doo doo doo
Surfer dude!

Went for a swim, doo doo doo doo doo
Went for a swim, doo doo doo doo doo
Went for a swim, doo doo doo doo doo
Went for a swim!

Lost an arm, doo doo doo doo doo
Lost an arm, doo doo doo doo doo
Lost an arm, doo doo doo doo doo
Lost an arm!

Lost a leg, doo doo doo doo doo
Lost a leg, doo doo doo doo doo
Lost a leg, doo doo doo doo doo
Lost a leg!

9-1-1, doo doo doo doo doo
9-1-1, doo doo doo doo doo
9-1-1, doo doo doo doo doo
9-1-1!

CPR, doo doo doo doo doo
CPR, doo doo doo doo doo
CPR, doo doo doo doo doo
CPR!

It's not working, doo doo doo doo doo
It's not working, doo doo doo doo doo
It's not working, doo doo doo doo doo
It's not working!

Reincarnation, doo doo doo doo doo
Reincarnation, doo doo doo doo doo
Reincarnation, doo doo doo doo doo
Reincarnation!

As a baby shark, doo doo doo doo doo
Baby shark, doo doo doo doo doo
Baby shark, doo doo doo doo doo
Baby shark!

15 August • Mermaid School • Clare Bevan

A lot less grisly than 'Baby Shark' is another marine-themed rhyme by Clare Bevan. Here she imagines the skills most important to that rarest of sea creatures – the mermaid.

What do mermaids learn at school?

How to sing beside a pool.
How to catch a flying fish.
How to grant an earth-child's wish.
How to chime a ship's old bell.
How to curl inside a shell.
How to win a sea-horse race.
How to swoop and dive and chase
Faster than the dolphin teams.
How to swim the silver beams
Of the small and misty moon.
How to play a magic tune.
How to tame a hungry shark.
How to find (when nights grow dark)
Hidden caves where treasures lie.
How to read a cloudy sky.
How to make a pearly ring.
How to mend a seabird's wing.
How to use a golden comb.
How to balance on the foam.
How to greet a friendly whale.
How to spin upon your tail.
How to twist and leap and turn . . .

This is what the mermaids learn.

16 August • Don't Call Alligator Long-Mouth till You Cross River • John Agard

This snappy verse is by John Agard, a British poet and playwright from Guyana, a country known as the 'Land of Many Waters' – but luckily for him, there are no alligators to be found in this part of South America.

Call alligator long-mouth
call alligator saw-mouth
call alligator pushy-mouth
call alligator scissors-mouth
call alligator raggedy-mouth
call alligator bumpy-bum
call alligator all dem rude word
but better wait
. . . till you cross river.

17 August • The Little Turtle • Vachel Lindsay

The American poet Vachel Lindsay (1879–1931), like E. V. Rieu, is another acclaimed twentieth-century writer who also wrote poems for children. Lindsay wrote what he called 'singing poetry' – verse designed to be chanted or sung – and has been credited with helping to keep poetry's oral tradition alive. 'The Little Turtle' was written in 1920, and is completely charming.

There was a little turtle.
He lived in a box.
He swam in a puddle.
He climbed on the rocks.

He snapped at a mosquito.
He snapped at a flea.
He snapped at a minnow.
And he snapped at me.

He caught the mosquito.
He caught the flea.
He caught the minnow.
But he didn't catch me.

18 August • The Gnu Song • Michael Flanders and Donald Swann

A gnu is a large animal also known as a wildebeest, and is found in the southernmost parts of Africa. The 'g' is silent, but due to the popularity of this song where the 'g' is pronounced for comic effect, many people think that a gnu is really called a *ger*-nu!

A year ago last Thursday I was strolling in the zoo
When I met a man who thought he knew the lot.
He was laying down the law about the habits of baboons
And how many spines a porcupine has got.
So I asked him, 'What's that creature there?'
He answered, 'Oh, it's a h'Elk.'
I might have gone on thinking that was true
If the animal in question hadn't put that chap to shame
And remarked, 'I h'aint a h'Elk, I'm a G-nu.'

'I'm a Gnu, I'm a Gnu
The g-nicest work of g-nature in the zoo
I'm a Gnu. How do you do?
You really ought to k-now w-ho's w-ho.
I'm a Gnu, spelt G-N-U
I'm g-not a Camel or a Kangaroo
So let me introduce
I'm g-neither man nor moose
Oh g-no, g-no, g-no, I'm a Gnu.'

I had taken furnished lodgings down at Rustington-on-Sea
Whence I travelled on to Ashton-under-Lyne (it was, actually)
And the second night I stayed there I was woken from a dream
That I'll tell you all about some other time.
Among the hunting trophies on the wall above my bed,
Stuffed and mounted, was a face I thought I knew;
A Bison? No, it's not a Bison.
An Okapi? Unlikely, really. A Hartebeest?
When I thought I heard a voice . . .

> 'I'm a Gnu, I'm a Gnu
> A g-nother Gnu.
> I wish I could g-nash my teeth at you
> I'm a Gnu. How do you do?
> You really ought to k-now w-ho's w-ho.
> I'm a Gnu, spelt G-N-U.
> Call me Bison or Okapi and I'll sue.
> G-nor am I the least like that dreadful Hartebeest,
> Oh, g-no, g-no, g-no,
> G-no, g-no, g-no, I'm a Gnu,
> G-no, g-no, g-no, I'm a Gnu.'

19 August • The Animal Fair • Anon.

Dating back to at least 1898, this entry takes us away from the sea and begins a run of fairground rhymes. It can be sung as a round, by four singers. When the first singer begins the second line, the second singer joins in from the beginning. Then, when the second singer reaches the second line, the third singer joins in from the beginning, and so on. Normally, 'monkey' is repeated by the earlier singers until the last one has reached the end.

We went to the animal fair,
The birds and the beasts were there,
The big baboon by the light of the moon
Was combing his golden hair.
The monkey fell out of his bunk,
And slid down the elephant's trunk,
The elephant sneezed – Atchoo! –
And fell on her knees,
And what became of the monkey,
Monkey, monkey, monkey, monkey?

20 August • Ride a Cock-Horse to Banbury Cross • Anon.

Although the earliest printing of this rhyme was not until the eighteenth century, it is believed to be much older. The author and philosopher Aldous Huxley (1894–1963) adapted the rhyme for his early science-fiction novel *Brave New World* (1932): 'Steptocock-Gee to Banbury T, to see a fine bathroom and W.C.' Banbury is a town in Oxford, where a bronze statue of this rhyme's fine lady was erected in 2005, with the lyrics on its plinth.

Ride a cock-horse to Banbury Cross
To see a fine lady upon a white horse;
With rings on her fingers and bells on her toes,
She shall have music wherever she goes.

21 August • As I Was Going to Banbury • Anon.

Banbury is famous for its seasonal fairs but its popularity in nursery rhymes is much to do with an enterprising printer J. G. Rusher – in the mid-nineteenth century – who kept substituting the name of his hometown in all the popular songs and ballads he reprinted.

As I was going to Banbury,
   Upon a summer's day,
My dame had butter, eggs, and fruit,
   And I had corn and hay.
Joe drove the ox, and Tom the swine,
   Dick took the foal and mare;
I sold them all – then home to dine,
   From famous Banbury fair.

22 August • Punch and Judy • Anon.

Punch and Judy is a traditional puppet show with roots in the sixteenth century. The two characters are always fighting. You wouldn't want this couple round for a dinner party.

Punch and Judy
   Fought for a pie,
Punch gave Judy
   A knock in the eye.

Says Punch to Judy,
   'Will you have any more?'
Says Judy to Punch,
   'My eye is too sore.'

23 August • Simple Simon Met a Pieman • Anon.

The association between pies and fairs continues in this next rhyme, which might be based on the patron saint of holy fools. St Simeon of Emesa lived in the sixth century, and, amongst other eccentricities, used to go around with a dead dog tied around his waist. Probably another character to cross off your dream dinner party list . . .

Simple Simon met a pieman,
 Going to the fair;
Said Simple Simon to the pieman,
 'Let me taste your ware.'

Says the pieman to Simple Simon,
 'Show me first your penny';
Says Simple Simon to the pieman,
 'Indeed I have not any.'

Simple Simon went a-fishing,
 For to catch a whale;
All the water he had got
 Was in his mother's pail.

Simple Simon went to look
 If plums grew on a thistle;
He pricked his fingers very much,
 Which made poor Simon whistle.

He went for water in a sieve
 But soon it all fell through;
And now poor Simple Simon
 Bids you all adieu.

24 August • O Dear, What Can the Matter Be? • Anon.

This nursery rhyme celebrates all the different treats you can buy at a fair. It was first collected between the 1770s and 1780s, in a compilation of Scots folk songs. In that manuscript, Johnny's at the *Newcastle* fair – giving Banbury a break.

O dear, what can the matter be?
Dear, dear, what can the matter be?
O dear, what can the matter be?
Johnny's so long at the fair.

He promised he'd buy a fairing should please me,
And then for a kiss, oh! He vowed he would tease me,
He promised he'd bring me a bunch of blue ribbons
To tie up my bonny brown hair.

And it's O dear, what can the matter be?
Dear, dear, what can the matter be?
O dear, what can the matter be?
Johnny's so long at the fair.

He promised to buy me a pair of sleeve buttons,
A pair of new garters that cost him but two pence,
He promised he'd bring me a bunch of blue ribbons
To tie up my bonny brown hair.

And it's O dear, what can the matter be?
Dear, dear, what can the matter be?
O dear, what can the matter be?
Johnny's so long at the fair.

He promised he'd bring me a basket of posies,
A garland of lilies, a garland of roses,
A little straw hat, to set off the blue ribbons
That tie up my bonny brown hair.

25 August • Let's Go to Kentucky • Anon.

In the circle game associated with this American rhyme, the circle dances around the child nominated as 'señorita', who performs the actions of shaking, rumbling and spinning round.

Let's go to Kentucky,
Let's go to the fair,
To see a señorita,
With flowers in her hair.
Shake it, shake it, shake it,
Shake it if you can;
And if you cannot shake it,
Then do the best you can.
Oh, rumble to the bottom,
Rumble to the top,
Round and round,
Round and round,
Until you cannot stop!

26 August • Banyan Tree • Anon.

Here's another dance song – this time from Jamaica, and written in patois (a regional dialect). The banyan is a special kind of tree. Rather than growing from the ground as other trees do, the banyan seed germinates in a crack in a host tree. The banyan tree's aerial roots then grow down from the host tree, towards the ground. Its unique appearance has given it significance in different parts of the world; for instance, it is the national tree of India, where its ever-expanding branches are taken to represent eternal life. Here, its falling roots provide a shelter for dancing.

Moonshine tonight, come mek we dance an sing,
Moonshine tonight, come mek we dance an sing.
Me deh rock so, yu deh rock so, under banyan tree,
Me deh rock so, yu deh rock so, under banyan tree.

Ladies mek curtsy, an gentlemen mek bow,
Ladies mek curtsy, an gentlemen mek bow.
Me deh rock so, yu deh rock so, under banyan tree,
Me deh rock so, yu deh rock so, under banyan tree.

Den we join hans and dance aroun an roun,
Den we join hans and dance aroun an roun.
Me deh rock so, yu deh rock so, under banyan tree,
Me deh rock so, yu deh rock so, under banyan tree.

27 August • Nellie the Elephant • Ralph Butler and Peter Hart

'Nellie the Elephant' was written in 1956 by Ralph Butler and Peter Hart, and its rhythm has since been used to teach people how to perform CPR. In 2005, the popular British children's author Jacqueline Wilson chose it as one of her Desert Island Discs.

To Bombay
A travelling circus came,
They brought an intelligent elephant
And Nellie was her name.
One dark night
She slipped her iron chain
And off she ran to Hindustan
And was never seen again.

Ohhhh . . .
Nellie the Elephant packed her trunk
And said goodbye to the circus,
Off she went with a trumpety-trump
Trump, trump, trump.
Nellie the Elephant packed her trunk
And trundled back to the jungle,
Off she went with a trumpety-trump
Trump, trump, trump.

The head of the herd was calling
Far, far away
They met one night in the silver light
On the road to Mandalay.

So Nellie the Elephant packed her trunk
And said goodbye to the circus,
Off she went with a trumpety-trump
Trump, trump, trump.

Night by night
She danced to the circus band.
When Nellie was leading the big parade
She looked so proud and grand.
No more tricks
For Nellie to perform,
They taught her how to take a bow
And she took the crowd by storm.

Nellie the Elephant packed her trunk
And said goodbye to the circus,
Off she went with a trumpety-trump
Trump, trump, trump.
Nellie the Elephant packed her trunk
And trundled back to the jungle,
Off she went with a trumpety-trump
Trump, trump, trump.

The head of the herd was calling
Far, far away
They met one night in the silver light
On the road to Mandalay.
So Nellie the Elephant packed her trunk
And said goodbye to the circus,
Off she went with a trumpety-trump
Trump, trump, trump.

28 August • Down by the Bay, where the Watermelons Grow • Anon.

This silly song has been sung around campfires for generations, encouraging children to make up further lines until they run out of rhyming ideas.

Down by the bay, where the watermelons grow,
Back to my home, I dare not go,
For if I do, my mother will say . . .
Did you ever see a moose, kissing a goose,
Down by the bay?

Down by the bay, where the watermelons grow,
Back to my home, I dare not go,
For if I do, my mother will say . . .
Did you ever see a whale, with a polka-dot tail,
Down by the bay?

Down by the bay, where the watermelons grow,
Back to my home, I dare not go,
For if I do, my mother will say . . .
Did you ever see a fly, wearing a tie,
Down by the bay?

Down by the bay, where the watermelons grow,
Back to my home, I dare not go,
For if I do, my mother will say . . .
Did you ever see a bear, combing his hair,
Down by the bay?

Down by the bay, where the watermelons grow,
Back to my home, I dare not go,
For if I do, my mother will say. . .
Did you ever see llamas, eating their pyjamas,
Down by the bay?

Down by the bay, where the watermelons grow,
Back to my home, I dare not go,
For if I do, my mother will say . . .
Did you ever see an octopus, dancing with a platypus,
Down by the bay?

Down by the bay, where the watermelons grow,
Back to my home, I dare not go,
For if I do, my mother will say . . .
Did you ever have a time, when you couldn't make a rhyme,
Down by the bay?

29 August • Take Me Out to the Ball Game • Jack Norworth

Written in 1908 by Jack Norworth to music by Albert von Tilzer, the chorus is considered America's unofficial baseball anthem. A 'sou' is a low-denomination coin, in turn-of-the-century slang.

Katie Casey was baseball mad,
Had the fever and had it bad.
Just to root for the home town crew,
Ev'ry sou, Katie blew.

On a Saturday her young beau
Called to see if she'd like to go
To see a show, but Miss Kate said, 'No,
I'll tell you what you can do . . .'

> Take me out to the ball game,
> Take me out with the crowd;
> Buy me some peanuts and Cracker Jack,
> I don't care if I never get back.
> Let me root, root, root for the home team,
> If they don't win, it's a shame.
> For it's one, two, three strikes, you're out,
> At the old ball game.

Katie Casey saw all the games,
Knew the players by their first names.
Told the umpire he was wrong,
All along, good and strong.

When the score was just two to two,
Katie Casey knew what to do.
Just to cheer up the boys she knew,
She made the gang sing this song:

> Take me out to the ball game,
> Take me out with the crowd;
> Buy me some peanuts and Cracker Jack,
> I don't care if I never get back.
> Let me root, root, root for the home team,
> If they don't win, it's a shame.
> For it's one, two, three strikes, you're out,
> At the old ball game.

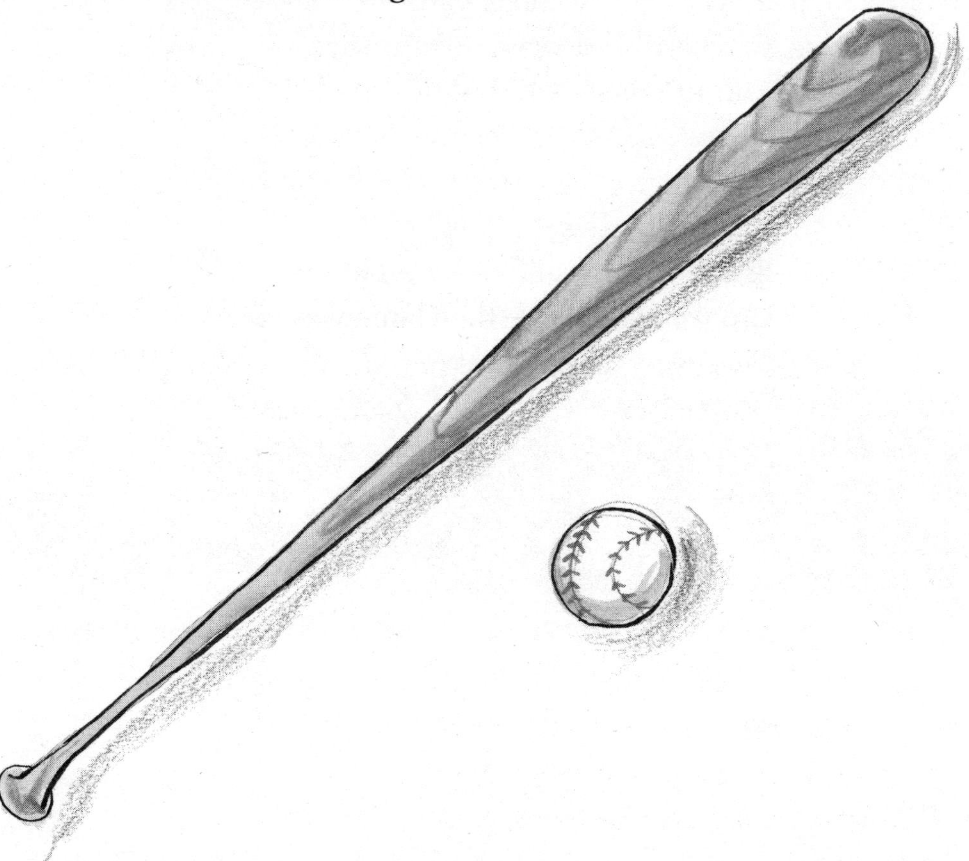

30 August • Brissit Brawnis and Brokin Banis (Bruised Bodies, Broken Bones) • Anon.

Ball games, however, haven't always been so civilised. These couplets are from a Middle Scots manuscript from the 1500s, from a time when football was far more aggressive. Medieval mob football was played in towns by two teams of any size. Aside from their feet, players could use sticks, hands or anything else, to move the ball – which was in fact usually an inflated pig's bladder.

Brissit brawnis and brokin banis,
Stryf discorde and waistie wanis,
Cruikit in eild syn halt with all;
Thir are the bewteis of the fute bale.

(original)

Bruised bodies, broken bones,
Strife, discord and deserted homes.
Crooked in old age then lameness too,
These are the beauties of football.

(translation)

31 August • In August, When the Days are Hot • Anon.

Sometimes, after all this sweltering outdoor fun, the only thing left to do is rest.

In August, when the days are hot,
I like to find a shady spot,
And hardly move a single bit –
And sit –
And sit –
And sit –
And sit!

Back to School

1 September • At Playschool • Rod Campbell

For the start of September, we celebrate the first day at playschool with a nursery rhyme by Rod Campbell.

Coat on your peg.
Meet Jill and Greg.
Draw a shy mouse.
Then build a house.
Go to your seat.
Now something to eat!

2 September • Head, Shoulders, Knees and Toes • Anon.

This is a lively one to act out together at the beginning of a school day.

Head, shoulders, knees and toes,
    Knees and toes.
Head, shoulders, knees and toes,
    Knees and toes
And eyes, and ears, and mouth and nose,
Head, shoulders, knees and toes,
    Knees and toes.

3 September • Monday's Child is Fair of Face • Anon.

Charles Addams, the cartoonist creator of *The Addams Family,* named the maudlin character Wednesday after this old fortune-telling rhyme. The fictional family have returned in a hit TV series by Tim Burton, who has even called the show *Wednesday*. Back to the rhyme in question, the favourable prophecy for Sunday's child reflects a superstition that can be traced back to medieval times.

> Monday's child is fair of face,
> Tuesday's child is full of grace,
> Wednesday's child is full of woe,
> Thursday's child has far to go,
> Friday's child is loving and giving,
> Saturday's child works hard for a living,
> And the child that is born on the Sabbath day
> Is bonny and blithe, and good and gay.

4 September • Sneeze on Monday, Sneeze for Danger • Anon.

An old superstition held that sneezing causes your soul to leave your body – hence the phrase 'bless you'. In some cultures, sneezing signifies that the gods have noticed you. In others, sneezing on your friend's threshold brings bad luck – or a hefty fine during the Covid pandemic. Yet perhaps the most complex superstitions are described in this proverbial rhyme, where the sneeze's meaning changes depending on the day of the week.

Sneeze on Monday, sneeze for danger;
Sneeze on Tuesday, kiss a stranger;
Sneeze on Wednesday, get a letter;
Sneeze on Thursday, something better;
Sneeze on Friday, sneeze for sorrow;
Sneeze on Saturday, joy for tomorrow.
Sneeze on Sunday before you break your fast,
You'll see your true love before a week is past.

5 September • Solomon Grundy • Anon.

This nursery rhyme depicts an entire life's journey within the course of a week, and has long been used to teach the days of the week to children.

Solomon Grundy,
Born on a Monday,
Christened on Tuesday,
Married on Wednesday,
Took ill on Thursday,
Worse on Friday,
Died on Saturday,
Buried on Sunday;
This is the end
Of Solomon Grundy.

6 September • One, Two, Three • Anon.

It's the time of year when the hashtag #BacktoSchool is trending. Today's entry begins a run of nursery rhymes which help children learn to count. While we can trace this rhyme back to the nineteenth century, there is a dispute over whether it is originally Irish or American – something typical of nursery rhymes, which tend to 'go viral', mutating over time.

One, two, three,
Mother finds a flea,
Puts it in the teapot
And makes a cup of tea.

The flea jumps out,
Mother gives a shout,
And down comes Father
With his shirt hanging out.

Four, five, six,
Father's in a fix,
He's got to find a billy goat
And hatch a few more chicks.

The chicks hatch out,
Father gives a shout,
And down comes Granny
With her hair sticking out.

Seven, eight, nine,
Granny's doing fine,
Scrubs all the children
And pegs them on the line.

The line gives way,
Granny shouts, 'Hey!'
'Wow!' cry the children
And they all run away.

7 September • This Old Man • Anon.

This nonsensical counting song appears to have arrived sometime in the early twentieth century, originally featuring the long-lost character Jack Jintle (instead of the old man who features here).

This old man, he played one,
He played knick-knack on my drum,
With a knick-knack paddy whack, give a dog a bone
This old man came rolling home.

This old man, he played two,
He played knick-knack on my shoe,
With a knick-knack paddy whack, give a dog a bone
This old man came rolling home.

This old man, he played three,
He played knick-knack on my knee,
With a knick-knack paddy whack, give a dog a bone
This old man came rolling home.

This old man, he played four,
He played knick-knack on my door,
With a knick-knack paddy whack, give a dog a bone
This old man came rolling home.

This old man, he played five,
He played knick-knack on my hide,
With a knick-knack paddy whack, give a dog a bone
This old man came rolling home.

This old man, he played six,
He played knick-knack on some sticks,
With a knick-knack paddy whack, give a dog a bone
This old man came rolling home.

This old man, he played seven,
He played knick-knack up in heaven,
With a knick-knack paddy whack, give a dog a bone
This old man came rolling home.

This old man, he played eight,
He played knick-knack on my plate,
With a knick-knack paddy whack, give a dog a bone
This old man came rolling home.

This old man, he played nine,
He played knick-knack on my spine,
With a knick-knack paddy whack, give a dog a bone
This old man came rolling home.

This old man, he played ten,
He played knick-knack once again,
With a knick-knack paddy whack, give a dog a bone
This old man came rolling home.

8 September • One, Two, Buckle my Shoe • Anon.

This counting rhyme provided Agatha Christie with the title for her detective novel *One, Two, Buckle My Shoe* (1940), and has been around since the eighteenth century. Similar rhymes have been found in French, German and Turkish. The fact its attention suddenly shifts to 'maids' after twelve suggests this version might in fact combine two different nursery rhymes.

One, two,
Buckle my shoe;
Three, four,
Knock at the door;
Five, six,
Pick up sticks;
Seven, eight,
Lay them straight;
Nine, ten,
A big fat hen;
Eleven, twelve,
Dig and delve;
Thirteen, fourteen,
Maids a-courting;
Fifteen, sixteen,
Maids in the kitchen;
Seventeen, eighteen,
Maids in waiting;
Nineteen, twenty,
My plate's empty.

9 September • One, Two, Three, Four, Five • Anon.

Carers of young children often use this popular counting rhyme as a fingerplay.

One, two, three, four, five,
Once I caught a fish alive,
Six, seven, eight, nine, ten,
Then I let it go again.

Why did you let it go?
Because it bit my finger so.
Which finger did it bite?
This little finger on the right.

10 September • Mosquito One • Anon.

This Caribbean counting rhyme refers to that late-summer menace: the mosquito. Despite their size, mosquitoes are in fact the deadliest animals on Earth – deadlier than sharks. 'Callaloo' is a green vegetable stew; in Jamaica it is eaten for breakfast, and in Trinidad – where this nursery rhyme originates – it is a national dish.

Mosquito one,
Mosquito two,
Mosquito jump in de callaloo.

Mosquito three,
Mosquito four,
Mosquito fly out de ol' man door.

Mosquito five,
Mosquito six,
Mosquito break up de ol' man bricks.

Mosquito seven,
Mosquito eight,
Mosquito open de ol' man gate.

Mosquito nine,
Mosquito ten,
Mosquito tickle de ol' man hen.

11 September • One Potato • Anon.

Counting becomes a game with this nursery rhyme. To play, one child makes two fists which they stack on top of each other for 'One potato / Two potato'. Another child then pops on their own potato fists for three and four – at which point the first child must begin taking their hands from the bottom of the stack to be potato five, and so on.

One potato
Two potato
Three potato
Four –
Five potato
Six potato
Seven potato
More.

12 September • The Animals Went in Two by Two • Anon.

Liverpool FC fans turned this well-known nursery rhyme into a chant about Spanish striker Fernando Torres (who played for Liverpool from 2007 to 2011): 'His armband proves he was a red, / Torres! Torres! / You'll never walk alone, he said, / Torres! Torres! / We brought the lad from sunny Spain, / He got the ball, he scored again . . .' The original, however, tells the story of Noah's Ark, common to all of the Abrahamic religions.

The animals went in two by two,
  Hurrah! Hurrah!
The animals went in two by two,
  Hurrah! Hurrah!
The animals went in two by two,
The elephant and the kangaroo.
And they all went into the ark
For to get out of the rain.

The animals went in three by three,
  Hurrah! Hurrah!
The animals went in three by three,
  Hurrah! Hurrah!
The animals went in three by three,
The wasp, the ant and the bumblebee.
And they all went into the ark
For to get out of the rain.

The animals went in four by four,
  Hurrah! Hurrah!
The animals went in four by four,
  Hurrah! Hurrah!
The animals went in four by four,
The great hippopotamus stuck in the door.
And they all went into the ark
For to get out of the rain.

The animals went in five by five,
  Hurrah! Hurrah!
The animals went in five by five,
  Hurrah! Hurrah!
The animals went in five by five,
They felt so happy to be alive.
And they all went into the ark
For to get out of the rain.

The animals went in six by six,
  Hurrah! Hurrah!
The animals went in six by six,
  Hurrah! Hurrah!
The animals went in six by six,
They turned out the monkey because of his tricks.
And they all went into the ark
For to get out of the rain.

The animals went in seven by seven,
  Hurrah! Hurrah!
The animals went in seven by seven,
  Hurrah! Hurrah!
The animals went in seven by seven,

The little pig thought he was going to heaven.
And they all went into the ark
For to get out of the rain.

The animals went in eight by eight,
  Hurrah! Hurrah!
The animals went in eight by eight,
  Hurrah! Hurrah!
The animals went in eight by eight,
The slithery snake slid under the gate.
And they all went into the ark
For to get out of the rain.

The animals went in nine by nine,
  Hurrah! Hurrah!
The animals went in nine by nine,
  Hurrah! Hurrah!
The animals went in nine by nine,
The rhino stood on the porcupine.
And they all went into the ark
For to get out of the rain.

The animals went in ten by ten,
  Hurrah! Hurrah!
The animals went in ten by ten,
  Hurrah! Hurrah!
The animals went in ten by ten,
And Noah said, 'Let's start again!'
And they all went into the ark
For to get out of the rain.

13 September • One-ery, Two-ery, Tickery, Seven • Anon.

Today's ditty is a nonsense rhyme for children who perhaps aren't fans of counting. It can also be used to decide who's 'it' for a game.

> One-ery, two-ery, tickery, seven,
> Hallibo, crackibo, ten and eleven,
> Spin, span, muskidan,
> Twiddle-um, twaddle-um, twenty-one.

14 September • One Man Went to Mow • Anon.

Here is a delightfully simple cumulative verse. Imagine how different this sounds around the world – in Spain, dogs don't say 'woof', but instead say 'guau'; in China, 'wang'; and Turkey, 'hev'.

One man went to mow, went to mow a meadow,
One man and his dog – Woof! – went to mow a meadow.

Two men went to mow, went to mow a meadow,
Two men, one man and his dog – Woof! – went to mow
a meadow.

Three men went to mow, went to mow a meadow.
Three men, two men, one man and his dog – Woof! – went
to mow a meadow.

Four men went to mow, went to mow a meadow,
Four men, three men, two men, one man and his dog –
Woof! – went to mow a meadow.

Five men went to mow, went to mow a meadow.
Five men, four men, three men, two men, one man and his
dog – Woof! – went to mow a meadow.

15 September • Five Little Ducks • Anon.

Moving on from counting, we come to the slightly trickier business of subtraction – beginning with this childhood favourite. There's a hand action to accompany each line; use your fingers to represent the numbers, and for 'over the hills' wave your hand. To show Mother Duck quacking, open and close your hand to represent her beak.

Five little ducks went swimming one day,
    Over the hills and far away.
Mother Duck said, 'Quack, quack, quack, quack,'
    But only four little ducks came back.

Four little ducks went swimming one day,
    Over the hills and far away.
Mother Duck said, 'Quack, quack, quack, quack,'
    But only three little ducks came back.

Three little ducks went swimming one day,
    Over the hills and far away.
Mother Duck said, 'Quack, quack, quack, quack,'
    But only two little ducks came back.

Two little ducks went swimming one day,
    Over the hills and far away.
Mother Duck said, 'Quack, quack, quack, quack,'
    But only one little duck came back.

One little duck went swimming one day,
    Over the hills and far away.
Mother Duck said, 'Quack, quack, quack, quack,'
    And all of the five little ducks came back.

16 September • Ten in the Bed • Anon.

This subtraction rhyme is a lively one for the end of the day. This is another not to try at home, unless you have a very big bed.

There were ten in the bed
And the little one said,
'Roll over, roll over.'
So they all rolled over
And one fell out . . .

There were nine in the bed
And the little one said,
'Roll over, roll over.'
So they all rolled over
And one fell out . . .

There were eight in the bed
And the little one said,
'Roll over, roll over.'
So they all rolled over
And one fell out . . .

There were seven in the bed
And the little one said,
'Roll over, roll over.'
So they all rolled over
And one fell out . . .

There were six in the bed
And the little one said,
'Roll over, roll over.'

So they all rolled over
And one fell out . . .

There were five in the bed
And the little one said,
'Roll over, roll over.'
So they all rolled over
And one fell out . . .

There were four in the bed
And the little one said,
'Roll over, roll over.'
So they all rolled over
And one fell out . . .

There were three in the bed
And the little one said,
'Roll over, roll over.'
So they all rolled over
And one fell out . . .

There were two in the bed
And the little one said,
'Roll over, roll over.'
So they all rolled over
And one fell out . . .

There was one in the bed
And the little one said,
'I've done it! I've done it!'

17 September • Five Currant Buns • Anon.

Groups of children play this subtraction game by substituting one of their own names for each verse.

Five currant buns in a baker's shop,
Round and fat with sugar on top.
Along came *Jack* with a penny one day,
Bought a currant bun and took it away.

Four currant buns in a baker's shop,
Round and fat with sugar on top.
Along came *Rosie* with a penny one day,
Bought a currant bun and took it away.

Three currant buns in a baker's shop,
Round and fat with sugar on top.
Along came *Eliza* with a penny one day,
Bought a currant bun and took it away.

Two currant buns in a baker's shop,
Round and fat with sugar on top.
Along came *Billy* with a penny one day,
Bought a currant bun and took it away.

One currant bun in a baker's shop,
Round and fat with sugar on top.
Along came *Nell* with a penny one day,
Bought a currant bun and took it away.

No currant buns in a baker's shop,
Round and fat with sugar on the top.
Along came *Romy* with a penny one day,
No currant buns, so *she* went right away.

18 September • Five Little Monkeys • Anon.

This inventive counting-down rhyme can also be used as a fingerplay. Hold up one hand and drop down one finger during each verse.

Five little monkeys walked along the shore;
  One went a-sailing,
  Then there were four.

Four little monkeys climbed up a tree;
  One of them tumbled down,
  Then there were three.

Three little monkeys found a pot of glue;
  One got stuck in it,
  Then there were two.

Two little monkeys found a currant bun;
  One ran away with it,
  Then there was one.

One little monkey cried all afternoon,
  So they put him in an airplane
  And sent him to the moon.

19 September • Ten Green Bottles • Anon.

In England during the Second World War, 'Ten Green Bottles' was turned into the jingoistic (and morbid!) children's song, which began 'There were ten German bombers in the air'!

Ten green bottles hanging on the wall,
Ten green bottles hanging on the wall,
And if one green bottle should accidentally fall,
There'd be nine green bottles hanging on the wall.

Nine green bottles hanging on the wall,
Nine green bottles hanging on the wall,
And if one green bottle should accidentally fall,
There'd be eight green bottles hanging on the wall.

Eight green bottles hanging on the wall,
Eight green bottles hanging on the wall,
And if one green bottle should accidentally fall,
There'd be seven green bottles hanging on the wall.

Seven green bottles hanging on the wall,
Seven green bottles hanging on the wall,
And if one green bottle should accidentally fall,
There'd be six green bottles hanging on the wall.

Six green bottles hanging on the wall,
Six green bottles hanging on the wall,
And if one green bottle should accidentally fall,
There'd be five green bottles hanging on the wall.

Five green bottles hanging on the wall,
Five green bottles hanging on the wall,
And if one green bottle should accidentally fall,
There'd be four green bottles hanging on the wall.

Four green bottles hanging on the wall,
Four green bottles hanging on the wall,
And if one green bottle should accidentally fall,
There'd be three green bottles hanging on the wall.

Three green bottles hanging on the wall,
Three green bottles hanging on the wall,
And if one green bottle should accidentally fall,
There'd be two green bottles hanging on the wall.

Two green bottles hanging on the wall,
Two green bottles hanging on the wall,
And if one green bottle should accidentally fall,
There'd be one green bottle hanging on the wall.

One green bottle hanging on the wall,
One green bottle hanging on the wall,
And if one green bottle should accidentally fall,
There'd be *no* green bottles hanging on the wall.

20 September • Five Little Speckled Frogs • Anon.

'Glub, glub' is a fairly accurate rendition of the noise that frogs make when eating. Because they have no teeth, they have to swallow their 'delicious' bugs whole.

Five little speckled frogs
Sat on a speckled log
Eating the most delicious bugs –
Yum, yum.
One jumped into the pool
Where it was nice and cool,
Then there were four green speckled frogs.
Glub, glub!

Four little speckled frogs
Sat on a speckled log
Eating the most delicious bugs –
Yum, yum.
One jumped into the pool
Where it was nice and cool,
Then there were three green speckled frogs.
Glub, glub!

Three little speckled frogs
Sat on a speckled log
Eating the most delicious bugs –
Yum, yum.
One jumped into the pool
Where it was nice and cool,
Then there were two green speckled frogs.
Glub, glub!

Two little speckled frogs
Sat on a speckled log
Eating the most delicious bugs –
Yum, yum.
One jumped into the pool
Where it was nice and cool,
Then there was one green speckled frog.
Glub, glub!

One little speckled frog
Sat on a speckled log
Eating the most delicious bugs –
Yum, yum.
He jumped into the pool
Where it was nice and cool,
Now there are no green speckled frogs.
Glub, glub!

21 September • Ten Fat Sausages • Anon.

Now we're subtracting by two . . .

Ten fat sausages sizzling in the pan,
Ten fat sausages sizzling in the pan.
One went POP! and the other went BANG!
Then there were eight fat sausages sizzling in the pan.

Eight fat sausages sizzling in the pan,
Eight fat sausages sizzling in the pan.
One went POP! and the other went BANG!
Then there were six fat sausages sizzling in the pan.

Six fat sausages sizzling in the pan,
Six fat sausages sizzling in the pan.
One went POP! and the other went BANG!
Then there were four fat sausages sizzling in the pan.

Four fat sausages sizzling in the pan,
Four fat sausages sizzling in the pan.
One went POP! and the other went BANG!
Then there were two fat sausages sizzling in the pan.

Two fat sausages sizzling in the pan,
Two fat sausages sizzling in the pan.
One went POP! and the other went BANG!
Then there were no fat sausages sizzling in the pan.

22 September • Multiplication is Vexation • Anon.

The Rule of Three – a mathematical rule for solving problems based on proportions – is no longer taught in English schools, thankfully.

Multiplication is vexation,
Division is as bad;
The Rule of Three doth puzzle me,
And practice drives me mad.

23 September • Do-Re-Mi • Oscar Hammerstein II

This famous song from *The Sound of Music* (1965) is actually about the so-called *solfège* system, an ancient technique to remember the notes of the musical scale by giving them each a name – but it's much more fun than that sounds!

Let's start at the very beginning,
A very good place to start.
When you read you begin with A-B-C,
When you sing you begin with do-re-mi.

Do-re-mi, do-re-mi
The first three notes just happen to be
Do-re-mi, do-re-mi . . .
Do-re-mi-fa-so-la-ti.
Let's see if I can make it easy.

Doe – a deer, a female deer
Ray – a drop of golden sun
Me – a name I call myself
Far – a long, long way to run
Sew – a needle pulling thread
La – a note to follow Sew
Tea – a drink with jam and bread
That will bring us back to Doe.

When you know the notes to sing,
You can sing most anything!

Doe – a deer, a female deer
Ray – a drop of golden sun
Me – a name I call myself
Far – a long, long way to run
Sew – a needle pulling thread
La – a note to follow Sew
Tea – a drink with jam and bread
That will bring us back to . . .

Doe – a deer, a female deer
Ray – a drop of golden sun
Me – a name I call myself
Far – a long, long way to run
Sew – a needle pulling thread
La – a note to follow Sew
Tea – a drink with jam and bread
That will bring us back to Doe!

24 September • Alphabet Song • Anon.

For many children in the English-speaking world, this basic alphabet song, sung to the same tune as 'Twinkle, Twinkle, Little Star', will be the first nursery rhyme they learn. It was published in the early nineteenth century in Boston, USA – which accounts for the rhyming of 'Z' with 'me'.

A, B, C, D, E, F, G,
H, I, J, K, L, M, N, O, P,
Q, R, S,
T, U, V,
W, X,
Y and Z.
Now I know my ABCs.
Next time won't you sing with me?

25 September • A Was an Apple-Pie • Anon.

This ABC rhyme has been around since the 1600s. (An 'ampersand' is a different type of letter, & you can guess which one it is & what it means!)

A was an apple-pie;
B bit it,
C cut it,
D dealt it,
E ate it,
F fought for it,
G got it,
H had it,
I inspected it,
J jumped for it,
K kept it,
L longed for it,
M mourned for it,
N nodded at it,
O opened it,
P peeped in it,
Q quartered it,
R ran for it,
S stole it,
T took it,
U upset it,
V viewed it,
W wanted it,
X, Y, Z and ampersand
All wished for a piece in hand.

26 September • A Was an Archer • Anon.

This rhyme is sometimes called 'Tom Thumb's Alphabet', after the little hero with big dreams in folklore (which perhaps explains the first line).

A was an archer, who shot at a frog,
B was a butcher, and had a great dog.
C was a captain, all covered with lace,
D was a drunkard, and had a red face.
E was an esquire, with pride on his brow,
F was a farmer, and followed the plough.
G was a gamester, who had but ill-luck,
H was a hunter, and hunted a buck.
I an innkeeper, who loved to carouse,
J was a joiner, and built up a house.
K was King William, once governed this land,
L was a lady, who had a white hand.
M was a miser, and hoarded up gold,
N was a nobleman, gallant and bold.
O was an oyster girl, and went about town,
P was a parson, and wore a black gown.
Q was a queen, who wore a silk slip,
R was a robber, and wanted a whip.
S was a sailor, and spent all he got,
T was a tinker, and mended a pot.
U was a usurer, a miserable elf,
V was a vintner, who drank all himself.
W was a watchman, and guarded the door,
X was expensive, and so became poor.
Y was a youth, that did not love school,
Z was a zany, a poor harmless fool.

27 September • A Nonsense Alphabet • Edward Lear

Edward Lear wrote many nonsense alphabets, and nearly all of them refer to King Xerxes – apart from this one, from 1877, where each letter of the alphabet comes up with an equally nonsensical cure.

A tumbled down, and hurt his Arm, against a bit of wood.
B said, 'My Boy, O! do not cry; it cannot do you good!'
C said, 'A Cup of Coffee hot can't do you any harm.'
D said, 'A Doctor should be fetched, and he would cure the arm.'
E said, 'An Egg beat up in milk would quickly make him well.'
F said, 'A Fish, if broiled, might cure, if only by the smell.'
G said, 'Green Gooseberry fool, the best of cures I hold.'
H said, 'His Hat should be kept on, keep him from the cold.'
I said, 'Some Ice upon his head will make him better soon.'
J said, 'Some Jam, if spread on bread, or given in a spoon!'
K said, 'A Kangaroo is here, – this picture let him see.'
L said, 'A Lamp pray keep alight, to make some barley tea.'
M said, 'A Mulberry or two might give him satisfaction.'
N said, 'Some Nuts, if rolled about, might be a slight attraction.'
O said, 'An Owl might make him laugh, if only it would wink.'
P said, 'Some Poetry might be read aloud, to make him think.'
Q said, 'A Quince I recommend, – a Quince, or else a Quail.'
R said, 'Some Rats might make him move, if fastened by their tail.'
S said, 'A Song should now be sung, in hopes to make him laugh!'
T said, 'A Turnip might avail, if sliced or cut in half!'
U said, 'An Urn, with water hot, place underneath his chin!'

V said, 'I'll stand upon a chair, and play a Violin!'
W said, 'Some Whisky-Whizzgigs fetch, some marbles and a ball!'
X said, 'Some double XX ale would be the best of all!'
Y said, 'Some Yeast mised up with salt would make a perfect plaster!'
Z said, 'Here is a box of Zinc! Get in, my little master!
'We'll shut you up! We'll nail you down! We will, my little master!
'We think we've all heard quite enough of this your sad disaster!'

28 September • Frère Jacques (Friar Jacques) • Anon.

This traditional French nursery rhyme has been around since at least the nineteenth century, and refers to a friar's obligation to ring the matins (or morning bells) of his church. The simplicity of its tune means it has been adapted all over the world. For instance, in the 1989 Tiananmen Square demonstration in Beijing, the rhyme was adapted as a political chant: 'Lying to the people, lying to the people, / Very strange, very strange.' For many English-speaking children it is the first (and possibly only!) French they will learn.

Frère Jacques, Frère Jacques,
Dormez-vous? Dormez-vous?
Sonnez les matines! Sonnez les matines!
Din, din, don. Din, din, don.

(original)

Friar Jacques, Friar Jacques,
Are you sleeping? Are you sleeping?
Ring the Matins bells! Ring the Matins bells!
Ding, dang, dong. Ding, dang, dong.

(translation)

29 September • Red and Yellow and Pink and Green • Anon.

This well-known nursery song has long been used by schoolchildren to remember the colours of the rainbow, albeit in the wrong order! The mnemonic 'Richard Of York Gave Battle In Vain', referring to the Duke of York's defeat at Wakefield in 1460, gives the correct order specified by Isaac Newton's colour circle: red, orange, yellow, green, blue, indigo, violet. Aside from muddling the colours, this nursery rhyme is also guilty of causing endless bafflement with the instruction to 'listen with your eyes, and sing everything you see'.

Red and yellow and pink and green
   Purple and orange and blue,
I can sing a rainbow, sing a rainbow,
   Sing a rainbow too.

Listen with your ears, listen with your eyes,
   And sing everything you see!
I can sing a rainbow, sing a rainbow,
   Sing along with me.

30 September • The Big Ship Sails through the Alley-Alley-O • Anon.

This rhyme for the last day in September divides opinion. Some believe the 'Alley-Alley-O' refers to the Manchester Ship Canal in England, partially due to the song's popularity in the Salford area. Others contend that the rhyme recounts the catastrophic sinking of the SS *Arctic* in late September 1854 – in this interpretation, the Alley-Alley-O is a nickname for the Atlantic Ocean.

The big ship sails through the Alley-Alley-O,
  Alley-Alley-O, Alley-Alley-O,
The big ship sails through the Alley-Alley-O,
  On the last day of September.

The Captain said, 'It will never never do,
  Never never do, never never do,'
The Captain said, 'It will never, never do,'
  On the last day of September.

The big ship sank to the bottom of the sea,
  Bottom of the sea, bottom of the sea,
The big ship sank to the bottom of the sea,
  On the last day of September.

We all dip our heads in the deep blue sea,
  The deep blue sea, the deep blue sea.
We all dip our heads in the deep blue sea,
  On the last day of September.

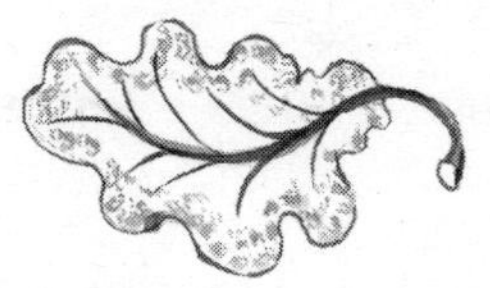

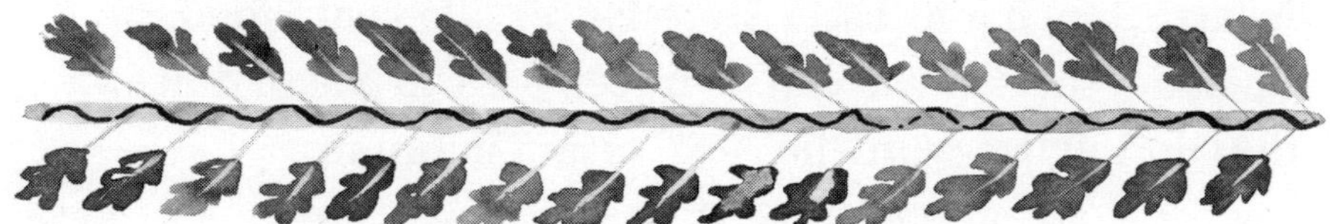

October

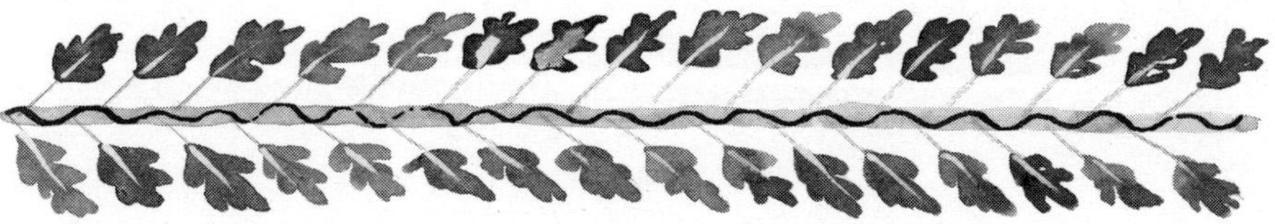

Food, Action Songs, Halloween

1 October • Jelly on a Plate • Anon.

October is a month for harvest festivities and feasting. A successful harvest sees storehouses filled with food. In England, this festival can be traced back to pagan times; the Old English word 'hærfest' meant autumn.

Jelly on a plate,
Jelly on a plate,
    Wibble, wobble,
    Wibble, wobble,
Jelly on a plate.

Sausage in a pan,
Sausage in a pan,
    Frizzle, frazzle,
    Frizzle, frazzle,
Sausage in a pan.

Baby on the floor,
Baby on the floor,
  Pick them up,
  Pick them up,
Baby on the floor.

2 October • Apples and Bananas • Anon.

This traditional North American children's song uses comedy to teach the vowel sounds.

I like to eat, eat, eat apples and bananas.
I like to eat, eat, eat apples and bananas.
I like to eat, eat, eat apples and bananas.
I like to eat, eat, eat apples and bananas.

Now let's make a long 'a' sound . . . ay-ples and ba-nay-nays.
I like to ate, ate, ate ay-ples and ba-nay-nays.
I like to ate, ate, ate ay-ples and ba-nay-nays.

Let's try a long 'e' sound . . . ee-ples and ba-nee-nees.
I like to eat, eat, eat ee-ples and ba-nee-nees.
I like to eat, eat, eat ee-ples and ba-nee-nees.

How about a long 'i' sound . . . i-ples and ba-nigh-nighs.
I like to ite, ite, ite i-ples and ba-nigh-nighs.
I like to ite, ite, ite i-ples and ba-nigh-nighs.

Great, let's sing it with a long 'o' sound . . . oh-ples and ba-no-nos.

I like to ote, ote, ote oh-ples and ba-no-nos.
I like to ote, ote, ote oh-ples and ba-no-nos.

I know, let's make an 'oo' sound . . . oo-ples and ba-noo-noos.

I like to oot, oot, oot, oo-pples and ba-noo-noos.
I like to oot, oot, oot, oo-pples and ba-noo-noos.

Apples and bananas, one more time!

I like to eat, eat, eat apples and bananas.
I like to eat, eat, eat apples and bananas.
I like to eat, eat, eat apples and bananas.
I like to eat, eat, eat apples and bananas.

3 October • Appley Dapply • Beatrix Potter

On the other side of the Atlantic, animal-lover Beatrix Potter (1866–1943) published two collections of nursery rhymes (*Appley Dapply* and *Cecily Parsley*), as well as writing nursery rhymes throughout her *Peter Rabbit* storybooks.

Appley Dapply, a little brown mouse,
Goes to the cupboard in somebody's house.

In somebody's cupboard
  There's everything nice,
Cake, cheese, jam, biscuits,
  – All charming for mice!

Appley Dapply has little sharp eyes,
And Appley Dapply is *so* fond of pies!

4 October • The King's Breakfast • A. A. Milne

The notable A. A. Milne, best known for his creation of the loveable teddy bear Winnie-the-Pooh, was also the author of many children's poems. 'The King's Breakfast' originally appeared in the Milne's collection *When We Were Young*, and concerns itself with very serious matters . . . the King is out of butter! Whatever shall he spread on his morning toast? Thus ensues a chain of requests up and down the ladder.

The King asked
The Queen, and
The Queen asked
The Dairymaid:
'Could we have some butter for
The Royal slice of bread?'
The Queen asked
The Dairymaid
The Dairymaid
Said, 'Certainly,
I'll go and tell the cow
Now
Before she goes to bed.'

The Dairymaid
She curtsied,
And went and told
The Alderney:
'Don't forget the butter for
The Royal slice of bread.'
The Alderney
Said sleepily:

'You'd better tell
His Majesty
That many people nowadays
Like marmalade
Instead.'

The Dairymaid
Said, 'Fancy!'
And went to
Her Majesty.
She curtsied to the Queen, and
She turned a little red:
'Excuse me,
Your Majesty,
For taking of
The liberty,
But marmalade is tasty, if
It's very
Thickly
Spread.'

The Queen said
'Oh!'
And went to
His Majesty:
'Talking of the butter for
The Royal slice of bread,
Many people
Think that
Marmalade
Is nicer.
Would you like to try a little

Marmalade
Instead?'

The King said,
'Bother!'
And then he said,
'Oh, deary me!'
The King sobbed, 'Oh, deary me!'
And went back to bed.
'Nobody,'
He whimpered,
'Could call me
A fussy man;
I only want
A little bit
Of butter for
My bread!'

The Queen said,
'There, there!'
And went to
The Dairymaid.
The Dairymaid
Said, 'There, there!'
And went to the shed.
The cow said,
'There, there!
I didn't really
Mean it;
Here's milk for his porringer,
And butter for his bread.'

The Queen took
The butter
And brought it to
His Majesty;
The King said,
'Butter, eh?'
And bounced out of bed.
'Nobody,' he said,
As he kissed her
Tenderly,
'Nobody,' he said,
As he slid down
The banisters,
'Nobody,
My darling,
Could call me
A fussy man—
BUT
I do like a little bit of butter to my bread!'

5 October • Pease-Pudding Hot • Anon.

Made only of split peas, salt, pepper and butter, pease-pudding would not be top of many menus today. Oddly enough, in twentieth-century Hollywood history, the iconic Marilyn Monroe movie *Some Like It Hot* (1959) took its name from this rhyme.

Pease-pudding hot,
Pease-pudding cold,
Pease-pudding in the pot,
  Nine days old.

Some like it hot,
Some like it cold,
Some like it in the pot,
  Nine days old.

6 October • One Day a Boy Went Walking • Anon.

Another ditty tells of even stranger culinary experiences than eating nine-day-old pease-pudding.

One day a boy went walking
  And walked into a store.
He bought a pound of sausages
  And put them on the floor.

The boy began to whistle.
  He whistled up a tune,
And all the little sausages
  Danced around the room.

7 October • Aiken Drum • Anon.

I'm not sure that there is a food rhyme that surpasses the bizarreness of 'Aiken Drum', a traditional Scottish nonsense song.

There was a man lived in the moon, lived in the moon, lived in the moon,
There was a man lived in the moon,
And his name was Aiken Drum;
And he played upon a ladle, a ladle, a ladle,
And he played upon a ladle,
And his name was Aiken Drum.

And his hat was made of good cream cheese, good cream cheese, good cream cheese,
And his hat was made of good cream cheese,
And his name was Aiken Drum.

And his coat was made of good roast beef, good roast beef, good roast beef,
And his coat was made of good roast beef,
And his name was Aiken Drum.

And his buttons were made of penny loaves, penny loaves, penny loaves,
And his buttons were made of penny loaves,
And his name was Aiken Drum.

His waistcoat was made of crust of pies, crust of pies, crust of pies,
His waistcoat was made of crust of pies,
And his name was Aiken Drum.

His breeches were made of haggis bags, haggis bags, haggis bags,
His breeches were made of haggis bags,
And his name was Aiken Drum.

There was a man in another town, another town, another town,
There was a man in another town,
And his name was Willy Wood;
  And he played upon a razor, a razor, a razor,
  And he played upon a razor,
  And his name was Willy Wood.

And he ate up all the good cream cheese, good cream cheese,
  good cream cheese,
And he ate up all the good cream cheese,
And his name was Willy Wood.

And he ate up all the good roast beef, good roast beef, good
  roast beef,
And he ate up all the good roast beef,
And his name was Willy Wood.

And he ate up all the penny loaves, penny loaves, penny loaves,
And he ate up all the penny loaves,
And his name was Willy Wood.

And he ate up all the good pie crust, good pie crust, good pie crust,
And he ate up all the good pie crust,
And his name was Willy Wood.

But he choked upon the haggis bags, haggis bags, haggis bags,
But he choked upon the haggis bags,
And that ended Willy Wood.

8 October • Polly Put the Kettle On • Anon.

The earliest printed record of this rhyme is in the novel *Barnaby Rudge* (1841), by the great Victorian novelist Charles Dickens (1812–1870). Given its subject matter, this is possibly the most British rhyme collected here.

Polly put the kettle on,
Polly put the kettle on,
Polly put the kettle on,
We'll all have tea.

Sukey take it off again,
Sukey take it off again,
Sukey take it off again,
They've all gone away.

Blow the fire and make the toast,
Put the muffins on to roast,
Who is going to eat the most?
We'll all have tea.

9 October • I'm a Little Teapot • Clarence Z. Kelley and George Sanders

On the topic of tea, we move on to this popular action rhyme. It was written in the era of Tin Pan Alley, originally to teach young children their first tap-dance moves.

I'm a little teapot,
Short and stout,
Here's my handle,
Here's my spout.
When I get a steam up,
Hear me shout:
Pick me up and pour me out!

10 October • Dance, Little Baby • Anon.

Today's rhyme calls to mind a Zimbabwean saying: 'If you can walk, you can dance; if you can talk, you can sing.'

Dance, little baby, dance up high:
Never mind, baby, mother is by;
Crow and caper, caper and crow,
There, little baby, there you go;
Up to the ceiling, down to the ground,
Backwards and forwards, round and round:
Dance, little baby, and mother shall sing,
With the merry gay coral, ding, ding-a-ding, ding.

11 October • Wind the Bobbin Up • Anon.

Nursery rhyme scholars Iona and Peter Opie traced this action rhyme back to the Netherlands in the 1890s. A 'bobbin' is a spool or reel for a spinning top.

Wind the bobbin up,
Wind the bobbin up,
Pull, pull, clap, clap, clap.
Wind it back again,
Wind it back again,
Pull, pull, clap, clap, clap,

Point to the ceiling,
Point to the floor,
Point to the window,
Point to the door,
Clap your hands together, one, two, three,
And place them gently upon your knee.

12 October • Mr Peter Rabbit had a Fly upon his Nose • Anon.

This song is, of course, inspired by Beatrix Potter's mischievous character, Peter Rabbit.

Mr Peter Rabbit had a fly upon his nose,
Mr Peter Rabbit had a fly upon his nose,
Mr Peter Rabbit had a fly upon his nose,
So he flipped it and he flopped it and the fly flew away.

Poor old poor old Peter Rabbit,
Poor old poor old Peter Rabbit,
Poor old poor old Peter Rabbit,
So he flipped it and he flopped it and the fly flew away.

13 October • Incy Wincy Spider • Anon.

Sometimes known as 'Itsy bitsy' rather than 'Incy wincy', this Sisyphean action rhyme is over a century old. The accompanying fingerplay works by touching your left thumb to your right index finger, and vice versa alternately, for the spider climbing. For 'down came the rain', you wiggle your fingers while lowering your hands, and for 'out came the sun' you spread both of your hands to create a circular sun above your head. Recently rapper Post Malone did a rap version of 'Itsy Bitsy Spider' in a fun segment of a YouTube morning show.

> Incy wincy spider climbed up the waterspout,
> Down came the rain and washed the spider out,
> Out came the sun and dried up all the rain,
> So Incy wincy spider climbed up the spout again.

14 October • Round and Round the Garden • Anon.

This tickling game is often presumed to be modern, as teddy bears were not commonplace until the twentieth century. However, it could be based on an older rhyme: 'Round about there / Sat a little hare / The bow-wows came and chased him / Right up there!' The accompanying fingerplay is to trace circles on a child's upturned palm and then gently tap fingers up their arms with each 'step', before tickling under the armpit.

Round and round the garden
Like a teddy bear;
One step, two step,
Tickle you under there!

15 October • Teddy Bear • Anon.

Make sure you do your stretches before you attempt this tricky skipping rhyme, which requires the player to act out each of the actions described between jumps on a rope. The skipper wins by spelling out 'goodnight' without missing a skip.

Teddy bear, teddy bear,
  Turn around.
Teddy bear, teddy bear,
  Touch the ground.

Teddy bear, teddy bear,
  Hands on head.
Teddy bear, teddy bear,
  Go to bed.

Teddy bear, teddy bear,
  Jump the stairs.
Teddy bear, teddy bear,
  Say your prayers.

Teddy bear, teddy bear,
  Turn out the light.
Teddy bear, teddy bear,
  Spell goodnight:
G.O.O.D.N.I.G.H.T.

16 October • Little Sally Water • Anon.

This delightful clapping game exists in many modifications; sometimes the weeping girl is 'Little Sally Ann / Sitting in the sand'; or or in the wonderful 1970 song 'Spirit in the Dark', the American soul singer Aretha Franklin calls her 'Sally Walker'.

Little Sally Water,
Sitting in a saucer,
Crying and a-weeping for someone to come.
Rise, Sally, rise, Sally,
Wipe your weeping eyes, Sally.
Fly to the East, Sally,
Fly to the West, Sally,
Fly to the one that you love the best.
Put your hands on your hips,
Let your backbone shake,
Shake it to the East,
Shake it to the West,
Shake it to the very one that you love the best.

17 October • The Wise Man Built his House upon the Rock • Anon.

Based on a parable that is told during the Sermon on the Mount (Matthew 7:24-27), this song has accompanying actions. *Wise* = point to forehead. *Built* = stack fists. *House* = steepled fingers. *Rock* = place fist in hand. *Rain came down* = wiggle fingers as they descend. *Floods came up* = raise wiggly fingers. *Firm* = fist in hand. *Foolish* = shake head while wagging finger. *Sand* = make a cross with your arms.

The wise man built his house upon the rock,
The wise man built his house upon the rock,
The wise man built his house upon the rock,
And the rain came tumbling down.

The rain came down and the floods came up,
The rain came down and the floods came up,
The rain came down and the floods came up,
And the house on the rock stood firm.

The foolish man built his house upon the sand,
The foolish man built his house upon the sand,
The foolish man built his house upon the sand,
And the rain came tumbling down.

The rain came down and the floods came up,
The rain came down and the floods came up,
The rain came down and the floods came up,
And the house on the sand went smash.

18 October • The Wheels on the Bus • Verna Hills

'The Wheels on the Bus' was written in 1939 by the Bostonian writer Verna Hills (1898–1990), but the wheels on the bus in her original version went round and round, 'over the city streets'.

The wheels on the bus go round and round,
Round and round, round and round.
The wheels on the bus go round and round,
    All day long.

The wipers on the bus go swish, swish, swish,
Swish, swish, swish, swish, swish, swish,
The wipers on the bus go swish, swish, swish,
    All day long.

The driver on the bus goes: 'Toot! Toot! Toot!'
'Toot! Toot! Toot! Toot! Toot! Toot!'
The driver on the bus goes, 'Toot! Toot! Toot!'
    All day long.

The conductor on the bus says: 'Hurry along please!'
'Hurry along please! Hurry along please!'
The conductor on the bus says: 'Hurry along please!'
    All day long.

The children on the bus make TOO MUCH NOISE!
TOO MUCH NOISE! TOO MUCH NOISE!
The children on the bus make TOO MUCH NOISE!
    All day long.

The babies on the bus fall fast asleep,
Fast asleep, fast asleep,
The babies on the bus fall fast asleep,
    All day long.

19 October • The Hokey Cokey • Anon.

Interestingly, this popular song is known as the 'Hokey Pokey' in America, Australia, Israel, Canada and South Africa; but 'hokey pokey' means honeycomb toffee in New Zealand, so there they call it the 'Hokey Tokey'. There are variants going as far back as the 1800s, and today it has been adapted into football chants by both Newcastle and West Ham fans. Some people believe that 'Hokey Cokey' is a corruption of 'hocus pocus', which is in turn a Protestant corruption of 'hoc est corpus meum' from the Catholic Mass.

You put your right arm in,
Your right arm out,
Your right arm in,
And you shake it all about.
You do the Hokey Cokey,
And you turn around,
That's what it's all about.

Oh, the Hokey, Cokey, Cokey!
Oh, the Hokey, Cokey, Cokey!
Oh, the Hokey, Cokey, Cokey!
Knees bend,
Arms stretch,
Ra! Ra! Ra!

You put your left arm in,
Your left arm out,
Your left arm in,
And you shake it all about.
You do the Hokey Cokey,

And you turn around,
That's what it's all about.

Oh, the Hokey, Cokey, Cokey!
Oh, the Hokey, Cokey, Cokey!
Oh, the Hokey, Cokey, Cokey!
Knees bend,
Arms stretch,
Ra! Ra! Ra!

You put your right leg in,
Your right leg out,
Your right leg in,
And you shake it all about,
You do the Hokey Cokey,
And you turn around,
That's what it's all about.

Oh, the Hokey, Cokey, Cokey!
Oh, the Hokey, Cokey, Cokey!
Oh, the Hokey, Cokey, Cokey!
Knees bend,
Arms stretch,
Ra! Ra! Ra!

You put your left leg in,
Your left leg out,
Your left leg in,
And you shake it all about,
You do the Hokey Cokey,
And you turn around,
That's what it's all about.

Oh, the Hokey, Cokey, Cokey!
Oh, the Hokey, Cokey, Cokey!
Oh, the Hokey, Cokey, Cokey!
Knees bend,
Arms stretch,
Ra! Ra! Ra!

You put your whole self in,
Your whole self out,
Your whole self in,
And you shake it all about,
You do the Hokey Cokey,
And you turn around,
That's what it's all about.

Oh, the Hokey, Cokey, Cokey!
Oh, the Hokey, Cokey, Cokey!
Oh, the Hokey, Cokey, Cokey!
Knees bend,
Arms stretch,
Ra! Ra! Ra!

20 October • Here We Go Looby-Loo • Anon.

This singing game is actually the ancestor of the Hokey Cokey (see above), and has been popular since at least the 1820s in America and the 1840s in England. A 'Looby' is someone clumsy, hence the instructions for dancing – though alternative lyrics have been found, especially in the North of England, which use 'Lubin' instead. 'Lubin' is apparently a nickname for a country bumpkin.

Here we go Looby-loo
Here we go Looby-light
Here we go Looby-loo
All on a Saturday night.
You put your right hand in,
You put your right hand out,
You give your hand a shake, shake, shake,
And turn yourself about.

Here we go Looby-loo,
Here we go Looby-light,
Here we go Looby-loo,
All on a Saturday night.
You put your left hand in,
You put your left hand out,
You give your hand a shake, shake, shake,
And turn yourself about.

Here we go Looby-loo,
Here we go Looby-light,
Here we go Looby-loo,
All on a Saturday night.

You put your right foot in,
You put your right foot out,
You give your foot a shake, shake, shake,
And turn yourself about.

Here we go Looby-loo,
Here we go Looby-light,
Here we go Looby-loo,
All on a Saturday night.
You put your left foot in,
You put your left foot out,
You give your foot a shake, shake, shake,
And turn yourself about.

Here we go Looby-loo,
Here we go Looby-light,
Here we go Looby-loo,
All on a Saturday night.
You put your whole self in,
You put your whole self out,
You give yourself a shake, shake, shake,
And turn yourself about.

Here we go Looby-loo,
Here we go Looby-light,
Here we go Looby-loo,
All on a Saturday night.

21 October • Did You Ever See a Lassie? • Anon.

To play this circle game, children form a circle and dance around one player who is the designated 'lassie'. When they reach 'Go this way and that', the child in the middle of the circle performs an action which all the other players must copy. Then the 'lassie' is swapped for another player, the 'laddie'. While the terms 'lassie' and 'laddie' seem to indicate a Scottish origin, the rhyme first appeared in the USA at the beginning of the twentieth century.

Did you ever see a lassie,
A lassie, a lassie?
Did you ever see a lassie
Go this way and that?
Go this way and that way,
Go this way and that way.
Did you ever see a lassie
Go this way and that?

Did you ever see a laddie,
A laddie, a laddie?
Did you ever see a laddie
Go this way and that?
Go this way and that way,
Go this way and that way.
Did you ever see a laddie,
Go this way and that?

22 October • One Finger, One Thumb • Anon.

This popular song can get you in a muddle, depending on how fast you sing and how much dancing you include. While singing the song, make sure to keep moving each body part it mentions! Choose your own action for chasing away the flies.

One finger, one thumb, keep moving
One finger, one thumb, keep moving
One finger, one thumb, keep moving
We'll all be merry and bright.

One finger, one thumb, one arm, keep moving
One finger, one thumb, one arm, keep moving
One finger, one thumb, one arm, keep moving
We'll all be merry and bright.

One finger, one thumb, one arm, one leg, keep moving
One finger, one thumb, one arm, one leg, keep moving
One finger, one thumb, one arm, one leg, keep moving
We'll all be merry and bright.

One finger, one thumb, one arm, one leg,
one nod of the head, keep moving
One finger, one thumb, one arm, one leg,
one nod of the head, keep moving
One finger, one thumb, one arm, one leg,
one nod of the head, keep moving
We'll all be merry and bright.

We'll all be merry and bright.

23 October • This is the Way the Ladies Ride • Anon.

For this song, try bouncing a small child on your knee, gently for the ladies, faster for the gentlemen, and then very rough galloping for the farmer. On the line 'Down into the ditch' at the end, the child is dangled between the knees. I wouldn't advise having a go at this immediately after eating.

This is the way the ladies ride:
Tri, tre, tre, tree,
Tri, tre, tre, tree!
This is the way the ladies ride:
Tri, tre, tre, tre, tri-tre-tre-tree!

This is the way the gentlemen ride:
Gallop-a-trot,
Gallop-a-trot!
This is the way the gentlemen ride:
Gallop-a-gallop-a-trot!

This is the way the farmers ride:
Hobbledy-hoy,
Hobbledy-hoy!
This is the way the farmers ride:
Hobbledy hobbledy-hoy!
Down into the ditch!

24 October • Miss Polly Had a Dolly • Anon.

This rhyme is used as a simple clapping rhyme between two children; on each of the repeated words they clap their hands together.

Miss Polly had a dolly
    Who was sick, sick, sick.
So she phoned for the doctor
    To come quick, quick, quick.
The doctor came
    With her bag and her hat,
And she knocked on the door
    With a rat-a-tat-tat.

She looked at the dolly
    And she shook her head,
And she said, 'Miss Polly,
    Put her straight to bed.'
She wrote on a paper
    For a pill, pill, pill,
'I'll be back in the morning
    With my bill, bill, bill.'

25 October • Helicopter Pilot Flying through the Air • Anon.

You don't have to be a professor of history to identify that this next entry is a contender for one of the newest in the book.

Helicopter pilot flying through the air,
Chop, chopper, chop, chopper,
    Chopper, chop chop!
Making all the people stop and stare,
Chop, chopper, chop, chopper,
    Chopper, chop chop!
Round and round goes the helicopter rotor,
Zoom! zoom! zoom! goes the helicopter motor.
Chop, chopper, chop, chopper,
    Chopper, chop chop!
    Chop, chopper,
    Chopper chop, chop!

26 October • Do Your Ears Hang Low? • Anon.

Brownies, Cubs, Scouts and some very gifted elephants have sung this silly song for generations.

Do your ears hang low?
Do they wobble to and fro?
Can you tie them in a knot?
Can you tie them in a bow?
Can you swing them over your shoulder
Like a regimental soldier?
Do your ears hang low?

27 October • Policeman Stops the Cars Like This • Anon.

This action song introduces children to the different members of the emergency services.

Policeman stops the cars like this
And lets them go like that.
He wears a pair of big black boots
And a tall policeman's hat.
He sometimes rides a motorbike
Or drives a Panda car.
Oh Mister Policeman, we are lost!
Please tell us where we are!

The fireman rings his bell like this
And climbs his steps like that.
He wears a pair of fireproof boots
And a fireproof fireman's hat.
His siren makes a dreadful noise
Each time he drives about.
Oh Mister Fireman, we're on fire!
Please come and put us out!

The man who drives the ambulance
Is ready day and night,
To come along and care for you
Inside his van of white.
And all the time he's on his way
His light is flashing blue.
Oh Mister Driver, we are hurt,
Please tell us what to do!

28 October • I Saw the Loch Ness Monster • Anon.

In nursery rhymes, anything is possible – in this account of the Loch Ness monster, she seems delightfully playful.

I saw the Loch Ness Monster
    As plainly as can be.
She lifted up her tiny little head
    And winked her eye at me.
She swam into the middle of the lake,
    She swam back to the shore,
Going up and down and up and down
    And up and down some more.

29 October • If You Ever Meet a Dinosaur • Anon.

This one has some great advice on tackling demons.

If you ever meet a dinosaur, tickle its toes,
Tickle its toes and wiggle its nose.
If you ever meet a dinosaur, tickle its toes.
Do you think you could do that?

If you ever meet a dragon, climb on its back,
Climb on its back and give it a pat.
If you ever meet a dragon, climb on its back.
Do you think you could do that?

If you ever meet a monster, tell it a joke,
Tell it a joke and give it a poke.
If you ever meet a monster, tell it a joke.
Do you think you could do that?

If you ever meet a ghost, give it a fright,
Give it a fright and turn on the light.
If you ever meet a ghost give it a fright.
Do you think you could do that?

30 October • In a Dark, Dark Wood • Anon.

This cumulative nursery rhyme masters the use of repetition to build suspense. It is thought that Halloween traditions relate to an ancient Celtic festival, when people would light fires to ward off ghosts.

In a dark, dark wood there was a dark, dark house,
And in that dark, dark house there was a dark, dark room,
And in that dark, dark room there was a dark, dark cupboard,
And in that dark, dark cupboard there was a dark, dark shelf,
And on that dark, dark shelf there was a dark, dark box,
And in that dark, dark box there was a GHOST!

31 October • Hey-How for Hallowe'en! • Anon.

In the Scottish Halloween tradition of 'guising' – which is similar to but pre-dates trick or treating – children don their fancy dress (to avoid detection by wicked ghouls, so legend has it) and go from door to door, trying to earn sweets or snacks in exchange for a joke, story or song.

Hey-how for Hallowe'en!
All the witches to be seen,
Some black, and some green,
Hey-how for Hallowe'en!

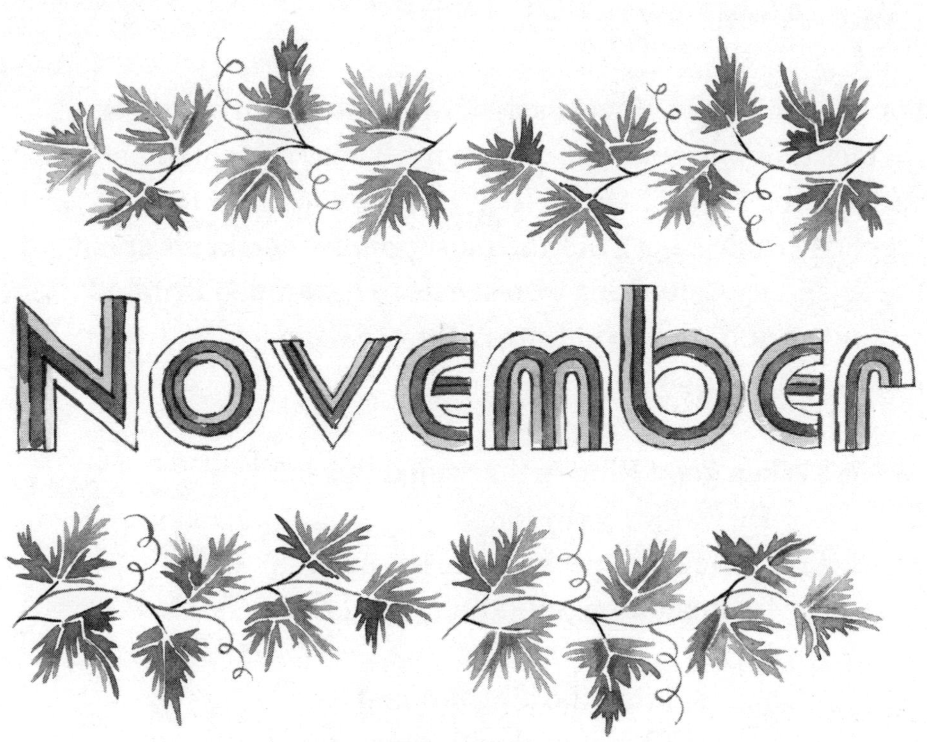

History, Divali, Thanksgiving

1 November • When Good King Arthur Ruled this Land • Anon.

For November, we travel back in time with a run of nursery rhymes that journey through history. Today's entry sometimes names King Henry I (1068–1135), or his successor King Stephen (1092–1154), but the most popular version is about the legendary Celtic king who seems to have ruled Britain around AD 500: the good King Arthur of Camelot (and Guinevere, his queen).

When good King Arthur ruled this land
    He was a goodly king;
He stole three pecks of barley-meal
    To make a bag-pudding.

A bag-pudding the king did make,
    And stuffed it well with plums;
And in it put great lumps of fat,
    As big as my two thumbs.

The king and queen did eat thereof,
    And noblemen beside;
And what they could not eat that night,
    The queen next morning fried.

2 November • Humpty Dumpty • Anon.

Although some say 'Humpty Dumpty' is about Richard III's death at the Battle of Bosworth (1485), others reckon it is just another riddle: the answer being that Humpty Dumpty is an egg. Equivalents can be found all over Europe; for instance, in Saxony, he is known as 'Hümpelken-Pümpelken'. Incidentally, Taylor Swift references the last lines in her song, 'The Archer' when she writes 'All the king's horses, all the king's men, / Couldn't put me together again'.

Humpty Dumpty sat on a wall,
Humpty Dumpty had a great fall.
    All the king's horses,
    And all the king's men,
Couldn't put Humpty together again.

3 November • In Fourteen Hundred Ninety-Two • Anon.

This rhyme's subject is one of history's most controversial figures, explorer/colonialist Christopher Columbus, and his accidental 'discovery' of America in 1492 while searching for a route to India – now that's a scenic route, if ever there was one.

In fourteen hundred ninety-two
Columbus sailed the ocean blue.

He had three ships and left from Spain;
He sailed through sunshine, wind and rain.

He sailed by night; he sailed by day;
He used the stars to find his way.

A compass also helped him know
How to find the way to go.

Ninety sailors were on board;
Some men worked while others snored.

Then the workers went to sleep,
And others watched the ocean deep.

Day after day they looked for land;
They dreamed of trees and rocks and sand.

October 12 their dream came true,
You never saw a happier crew!

'Indians! Indians!' Columbus cried;
His heart was filled with joyful pride.

But 'India' the land was not;
It was the Bahamas, and it was hot.

The Arakawa natives were very nice;
They gave the sailors food and spice.

Columbus sailed on to find some gold
To bring back home, as he'd been told.

He made the trip again and again,
Trading gold to bring to Spain.

The first American? No, not quite.
But Columbus was brave, and he was bright.

4 November • Divorced, Beheaded, Died • Anon.

Known by almost every British schoolchild, this rhyme helps us to remember the unhappy fates of each of Henry VIII's six wives in Tudor England in the 1500s. The accompanying mnemonic, 'Arrogant boys seem clever, Howard particularly', helps with the order of their names: Catherine of Aragon; Anne Boleyn; Jane Seymour; Anne of Cleves; Catherine Howard; Catherine Parr.

Divorced,
Beheaded,
Died.
Divorced,
Beheaded,
Survived.

5 November • Remember, Remember the Fifth of November • Anon.

The annual celebration of Bonfire Night falls on the anniversary of Guy Fawkes's failed Gunpowder Plot in 1605, after which he was put to a gruesome public death for treason – certainly one of the stranger British customs, when you think about it. Here the lesser-known additional verses are included.

Remember, remember
The Fifth of November,
Gunpowder treason and plot;
I see no reason
Why gunpowder treason
Should ever be forgot.

Guy Fawkes, Guy Fawkes, 'twas his intent,
To blow up the King and the Parliament.
Three-score barrels of powder blow,
Poor old England to overthrow.

By God's providence he was catched
With a dark lantern and lighted match.
Holler boys, holler boys,
Make the bells ring,
Holler boys, holler boys,
God save the King!

6 November • Georgie Porgie • Anon.

This rhyme is believed to refer to the very unpopular Stuart courtier George Villiers, Duke of Buckingham (1592–1628), and has been used to tease many a child called George ever since.

Georgie Porgie, pudding and pie,
Kissed the girls and made them cry;
When the boys came out to play,
Georgie Porgie ran away.

7 November • There was a Monkey Climbed a Tree • Anon.

George 'Georgie Porgie' Villiers's unpopularity soared with his disastrous expedition to Cadiz, Spain, in 1626. The final two lines of this rhyme are thought to allude to Buckingham's failure.

There was a monkey climbed a tree,
When he fell down, then down fell he.

There was a crow sat on a stone,
When he was gone, then there was none.

There was an old wife did eat an apple,
When she ate two, she ate a couple.

There was a horse going to the mill,
When he went on, he stood not still.

There was a butcher cut his thumb,
When it did bleed, then blood did come.

There was a lackey ran a race,
When he ran fast, he ran apace.

There was a cobbler clouding shoon,
When they were mended, they were done.

There was a chandler making candle,
When he them stripped, he did them handle.

There was a navy went to Spain,
When it returned, it came again.

8 November • As I Was Going by Charing Cross • Anon.

Charles I lost his head – literally, I don't mean he just got very upset – on 30 January 1649 after the axe-happy Parliamentarians defeated him and his Royalist supporters in the English Civil War. He and his horse are described as 'black' here, either because of the dark colour of their hair in life, or because the statue's brass had tarnished over time. The statue of him in this rhyme had originally been placed in a country garden in Roehampton, then sold to a metalsmith for breaking up during the Civil War. Instead, the metalsmith kept it hidden until the Restoration and in 1675 it was moved to Charing Cross, the centrepoint of London, where it stands – still very black – to this day.

As I was going by Charing Cross,
I saw a black man upon a black horse;
They told me it was King Charles the First –
Oh dear, my heart was ready to burst!

9 November • High Diddle Ding, Did You Hear the Bells Ring? • Anon.

The English Civil War started in 1642. This rhyme is either about the outbreak of the war, or the Restoration of the Monarchy in 1660, when Parliament soldiers went to offer Charles II (the exiled son of Charles I) the crown.

High diddle ding, did you hear the bells ring?
The parliament soldiers are gone to the king.
Some they did laugh, and some they did cry,
To see the parliament soldiers go by.

10 November • Little General Monk • Anon.

It seems likely this next entry is about the famous Stuart-era soldier General George Monck (1608–1670), who played a key role in the Restoration of the Monarchy. However, its resemblance stops at his name, as Monck actually died from fluid retention, otherwise known as dropsy.

Little General Monk
Sat upon a trunk,
Eating a crust of bread;
There fell a hot coal
And burnt in his clothes a hole,
Now little General Monk is dead.

11 November • Ring-a-Ring-a-Roses • Anon.

Though it has been discredited, the association of this action rhyme with the Great Plague of London in 1665 has become part of the English popular imagination. This is all the more fascinating when you consider how modern this interpretation is, having only gained traction in the twentieth century. The foreign and nineteenth-century versions imply that the fall described was originally a curtsy.

Ring-a-ring-a-roses
A pocket full of posies.
  A-tishoo! A-tishoo!
We all fall down.

Picking up the daisies
Picking up the daisies.
  A-tishoo! A-tishoo!
We all stand up.

12 November • London's Burning • Anon.

'London's Burning' is often sung as a round. It refers to the Great Fire of London in 1666, in which no more than six people are thought to have lost their lives, but seventy per cent of London burned to the ground.

London's burning, London's burning.
Fetch the engines, fetch the engines.
Fire, fire! Fire, fire!
Pour on water, pour on water.

13 November • I am Queen Anne • Anon.

Five years after Queen Anne came to the throne, she oversaw the 1707 Act of Union, which turned Scotland and England into the single sovereign state of Great Britain. So it feels somewhat unfair that she is 'chiefly famed for being dead'.

I am Queen Anne, of whom 'tis said
I'm chiefly famed for being dead.
Queen Anne, Queen Anne, she sits in the sun,
As fair as a lily, as brown as a bun.

14 November • The Lion and the Unicorn • Anon.

When Queen Anne unified England and Scotland, there was a big decision to be made on how to amalgamate the English and Scottish coats of arms. This rhyme appeared shortly afterwards, in William King's satirical text, *Useful Transactions in Philosophy* (1708–9). The lion, which was the English symbol, is considered to have beaten the Scottish unicorn because in the new coat of arms it is the lion who wears the crown.

The lion and the unicorn
   Were fighting for the crown;
The lion beat the unicorn
   All round about the town.
Some gave them white bread,
   Some gave them brown;
Some gave them plum cake
   And drummed them out of town.

15 November • The Grand Old Duke of York • Anon.

Prince Frederick, Duke of York and Albany (1763–1827) might never have been so famous, were it not for him being ridiculed (possibly unfairly!) in our next rhyme. Despite the Netherlands being famously flat with a distinct lack of hills, this is how the Duke of York's failed invasion of Holland in 1799 has been remembered.

Oh, the grand old Duke of York,
He had ten thousand men;
He marked them up to the top of the hill,
And he marched them down again.
And when they were up, they were up,
And when they were down, they were down,
And when they were only half-way up,
They were neither up nor down.

16 November • Yankee Doodle Came to Town • Anon.

Careful when you call people names: you never know what might come back to bite you. The word 'Yankee' is believed to have derived from the Cherokee word 'eankke', meaning 'coward'. During the American War of Independence, the British used this song to mock the 'Yankee' soldiers as unrefined colonial subjects. However, it quickly became popular with the so-called Yankees themselves, and the Americans actually played the song when the British Army came to sign the surrender documents that gave America its Independence in 1776.

Yankee Doodle came to town,
   Riding on a pony;
He stuck a feather in his cap
   And called it macaroni.

17 November • Ole Man Page'll Be in a Turble Rage • Anon.

This African American rhyme recounts an anecdote from the American Civil War (1861–1865), according to folklorist Thomas W. Talley (1870–1952). The anecdote follows that Yankee soldiers stole a slave-owner's geese and returned a single cent as 'pay'. Geese were symbolically important during this period; because they fly north to Canada, they could be used as guides for enslaved people fleeing to the northern free states.

Ole man Page'll be in a turble rage,
W'en he finds out, it'll raise his dander.
Yankee soldiers bought his geese, fer one cent a-piece,
An' sent de pay home by de gander.

18 November • Here We Go Round the Mulberry Bush • Anon.

In the 1700s and 1800s, the British cultivated mulberry trees to encourage silkworm habitation, in an attempt to replicate the success of the Chinese silk trade. However, the mulberry tree is sensitive to frost and harsh winters, so all attempts failed. The repeated refrain 'On a cold and frosty morning' suggests this rhyme might be satirizing the endeavour.

Here we go round the mulberry bush,
The mulberry bush, the mulberry bush,
Here we go round the mulberry bush,
On a cold and frosty morning.

This is the way we wash our hands,
Wash our hands, wash our hands,
This is the way we wash our hands,
On a cold and frosty morning.

This is the way we wash our clothes,
Wash our clothes, wash our clothes,
This is the way we wash our clothes,
On a cold and frosty morning.

19 November • Follow the Drinking Gourd • Anon.

This African American spiritual was used in the Underground Railroad. The 'drinking gourd' is another name for the constellation known as the Plough or the Big Dipper, and from the southern states of America it points north. Hence those fleeing slavery were instructed to 'follow the drinking gourd' if lost, as it would lead them to the northern states – and freedom.

Follow the drinking gourd
When the sun comes back,
And the first quail calls,
Follow the drinking gourd.
The old man is awaiting for to carry you to freedom
If you follow the drinking gourd.
  Follow the drinking gourd,
  Follow the drinking gourd,
  For the old man is awaiting for to carry you to freedom
  If you follow the drinking gourd.

The river bank will make a mighty good road,
The dead trees show you the way.
Left foot, peg foot, travelling on,
Follow the drinking gourd.
  Follow the drinking gourd,
  Follow the drinking gourd,
  For the old man is awaiting for to carry you to freedom
  If you follow the drinking gourd.

The river ends between two hills,
Follow the drinking gourd,
There's another river on the other side,
Follow the drinking gourd.
    Follow the drinking gourd,
    Follow the drinking gourd,
    For the old man is awaiting for to carry you to freedom
    If you follow the drinking gourd.

Where the great big river meets the little river
Follow the drinking gourd.
The old man is awaiting for to carry you to freedom
If you follow the drinking gourd.

20 November • The Queen of Hearts • Anon.

Lewis Carroll's *Alice's Adventures in Wonderland* (1865) popularized this childhood favourite, which may be subtly mocking Queen Victoria (1819–1901). In Carroll's book, the Queen of Hearts is foul-tempered and obsessed with beheading, while the King of Hearts quietly pardons his subjects when she is not looking. In the rhyme that inspired his characters, though, the King is less forgiving . . .

The Queen of Hearts
She made some tarts,
All on a summer's day;
The Knave of Hearts
He stole those tarts,
And took them clean away.

The King of Hearts
Called for the tarts,
And beat the knave full sore;
The Knave of Hearts
Brought back the tarts,
And vowed he'd steal no more.

21 November • Two Little Boys • Edward Madden

This heartrending song was written in 1902 by Edward Madden, with music by Theodore Morse. Some people believe it refers to the Second Boer War (1899–1902), others claim it is more likely about the American Civil War; but the theme of staying loyal to one's friends, even in the most hostile circumstances, is universal.

Two little boys
Had two little toys,
Each had a wooden horse;
Gaily they played
Each summer's day –
Warriors both of course.
One little chap
Then had a mishap,
Broke off his horse's head;
Cried for his toy,
Then cried for joy
As his young playmate said:

'Did you think I would leave you crying
When there's room on my horse for two?
Climb up here, Jack, we'll soon be flying;
I can go just as fast with two.
When we grow up we'll both be soldiers,
And our horses will not be toys;
And I wonder if we'll remember
When we were two little boys.'

Long years passed,
War came so fast;
Bravely they marched away.
Cannons roared loud
And in the mad crowd
Wounded and dying lay.
Up went a shout –
A horse dashes out,
Out from the ranks so blue,
Galloped away
To where Joe lay,
And then came a voice he knew:

'Did you think I would leave you dying
When there's room on my horse for two?
Climb up here, Joe, we'll soon be flying
Back to the ranks so blue.
Do you know, Joe, I'm all a-tremble,
Perhaps it's the battle's noise;
But I think it's that I remember
When we were two little boys.'

22 November • Good-Bye-Ee! • R. P. Weston and Bert Lee

The songwriters R. P. Weston and Bert Lee were apparently inspired to write this First World War music-hall song when they saw a group of factory girls calling out 'goodbye' to soldiers marching to London's Victoria station, on their way to the fighting fields of France.

Good-bye-ee! Good-bye-ee!
Wipe the tear, baby dear, from your eye-ee.
Tho' it's hard to part I know,
I'll be tickled to death to go.
Don't cry-ee! Don't sigh-ee!
There's a silver lining in the sky-ee.
Bonsoir, old thing! Cheerio! Chin-chin!
Nah-poo! Toodle-oo! Good-bye-ee!

23 November • Willie, Willie, Harry, Steve • Anon.

This impressive mnemonic verse, of which several alternatives exist, is used for remembering the order of English monarchs from William the Conqueror to Elizabeth II. It was adapted into 'The Monarch's Song' in the TV series *Horrible Histories*. 'Dick the bad' is Shakespeare's villain, Richard III; and 'Ned the lad' is Edward VI, who died young after having been king for only six years. Another mnemonic is used to remember the royal dynasties: 'No Plan Like Yours To Study History Wisely' (Norman, Plantagenet, Lancaster, York, Tudor, Stuart, Hanover, Windsor). See if you can find a way of adding Charles III ('Charlie three'?) to bring it up to date.

Willie, Willie, Harry, Steve,
Harry, Dick, John, Harry three;
One two three Neds, Richard two,
Harrys four five six – then who?
Edwards four five, Dick the bad,
Harrys (twain), Ned six (the lad);
Mary, Bessie, James you ken,
Then Charlie, Charlie, James again;
Will and Mary, Anna Gloria,
Georges four, Will four, Victoria;
Edward seven, George and Ted,
George the sixth, now Liz instead.

24 November • Lock In, Lock Up, All Lock Down • Floella Benjamin

Here is a brand-new nursery rhyme by Floella Benjamin: a performer, presenter, writer, and the first Trinidadian in the House of Lords. She has written this rhyme about life during the Covid pandemic especially for this book!

Lock in, Lock up, all Lock Down
Peer through the window, wave to the town
Lock in, Lock up, all Lock Down
Streets are empty, everyone's flown

Lock in, Lock up, all Lock Down
Doctor says numbers have grown
Lock in, Lock up, all Lock Down
Keep on smiling, try not to groan

Lock in, Lock up, all Lock Down
Everyone tries hard not to moan
Lock in, Lock up, all Lock Down
One day soon we can all leave home.

25 November • Remember, Remember • Brian Bilston

To end our run of history, Brian Bilston has written us a comic rhyme that tries to sum up all the facts and figures.

Remember, remember
The Fourth of November,
Soap powder, treacle and plot.
It walked in a puddle –
I've got in a muddle . . .
Hey diddle, dickory dock.

Remember, remember
The Twelfth of November,
It had ten thousand men.
And Little Boy Blue
Moved into a shoe . . .
No, I've got it wrong again.

Remember, remember,
The Third of September,
How does your garden grow?
With puppy dog's tails
And sugar-spiced snails . . .
No, no, no, no, no.

It's the Fifth of October,
The cow has jumped over
Little Miss Pudding and Pie.
A-tisket, atishoo,
My memory's an issue,
Oh, what a dull boy am I.

26 November • It is Divali, the Festival of Light • Anon.

Divali, or the Festival of Light, is celebrated by Hindus, Sikhs, Jains and some Buddhists, beginning on the fifteenth day of the Hindu lunar month Kartka (sometime between October and November). It is associated with Lakshmi, the Hindu goddess of prosperity. Families decorate their homes with 'divas' – oil lamps.

> It is Divali, the festival of light,
> Every house has divas that shine so bright.
> Even the stars from the heavens come down below
> To add sparkle to this pretty sight.

27 November • The New-England Boy's Song about Thanksgiving Day • Lydia Maria Child

The American festival of Thanksgiving is held on the last Thursday of November each year. This celebratory song was written by the poet Lydia Maria Child (1802–1880), a remarkable woman who lived in America in the nineteenth century and wrote the first comprehensive history of American slavery.

Over the river, and through the wood,
To grandfather's house we go;
The horse knows the way,
To carry the sleigh,
Through the white and drifted snow.

Over the river, and through the wood,
To grandfather's house away!
We would not stop
For doll or top,
For 'tis Thanksgiving Day.

Over the river, and through the wood,
Oh, how the wind does blow!
It stings the toes,
And bites the nose,
As over the ground we go.

Over the river, and through the wood,
With a clear blue winter sky;
The dogs do bark,
And children hark,
As we go jingling by.

Over the river, and through the wood,
To have a first-rate play;
Hear the bells ring
'Ting-a-ling-ding!'
Hurrah for Thanksgiving day!

Over the river, and through the wood —
No matter for winds that blow;
Or if we get,
The sleigh upset,
Into a bank of snow.

Over the river, and through the wood,
To see little John and Ann;
We will kiss them all,
And play snow-ball,
And stay as long as we can.

Over the river, and through the wood,
Trot fast, my dapple grey!
Spring over the ground,
Like a hunting hound,
For 'tis Thanksgiving day!

Over the river, and through the wood,
And straight through the barn-yard gate;
We seem to go
Extremely slow,
It is so hard to wait.

Over the river, and through the wood,
Old Jowler hears our bells;
He shakes his pow,
With a loud 'bow-wow',
And thus the news he tells.

Over the river, and through the wood –
When grandmother sees us come,
She will say, 'Oh dear,
The children are here,
Bring a pie for every one.'

Over the river, and through the wood –
Now grandmother's cap I spy!
Hurra for the fun!
Is the pudding done?
Hurrah for the pumpkin pie!

28 November • Johnny Appleseed • Anon.

This is another rhyme for Thanksgiving. The Johnny Appleseed of this rhyme was a real man called John Chapman (1774–1845). He earned his nickname by introducing apple trees to large parts of America, and soon after became a national legend.

Oh, the Lord is good to me,
And so I thank the Lord,
For giving me the things I need:
The sun and the rain and the apple seed.
    The Lord is good to me,
    Johnny Appleseed!

Oh, and every seed I sow
Will grow into a tree,
And someday there'll be apples there,
For everyone in the world to share.
    Oh, the Lord is good to me,
    Johnny Appleseed!

Oh, the earth is good to me,
And so I tha'k the earth,
For giving me the things I need:
The sun and the rain and the apple seed.
    The earth is good to me,
    Johnny Appleseed.

29 November • Peter, Peter, Pumpkin Eater • Anon.

Alongside giving thanks, another of Thanksgiving's traditional customs is pumpkin eating.

Peter, Peter, pumpkin eater,
Had a wife but couldn't keep her;
He put her in a pumpkin shell
And there he kept her very well.

Peter, Peter, pumpkin eater,
Had another and didn't love her;
Peter learned to read and spell,
And then he loved her very well.

30 November • Jingle Bells • James Lord Pierpont

Whilst 'Jingle Bells' is best known as a Christmas song, it was in fact written to celebrate the Thanksgiving 'jingle bell races' in New England. It is also notable as the first song to be broadcast from space, during a NASA Project Gemini mission.

Dashing through the snow
In a one-horse open sleigh,
O'er the fields we go
Laughing all the way.
Bells on bobtail ring,
Making spirits bright,
What fun it is to ride and sing
A sleighing song tonight! Oh!

  Jingle bells, jingle bells,
  Jingle all the way.
  Oh! what fun it is to ride
  In a one-horse open sleigh. Hey!
  Jingle bells, jingle bells,
  Jingle all the way;
  Oh! what fun it is to ride
  In a one-horse open sleigh.

A day or two ago
I thought I'd take a ride,
And soon, Miss Fanny Bright
Was seated by my side.
The horse was lean and lank,
Misfortune seemed his lot,
He got into a drifted bank
And then we got upsot.

Jingle bells, jingle bells,
Jingle all the way.
Oh! what fun it is to ride
In a one-horse open sleigh. Hey!
Jingle bells, jingle bells,
Jingle all the way;
Oh! what fun it is to ride
In a one-horse open sleigh.

A day or two ago,
The story I must tell,
I went out on the snow,
And on my back I fell;
A gent was riding by
In a one-horse open sleigh;
He laughed as there I sprawling lie,
But quickly drove away. Ah!

Jingle bells, jingle bells,
Jingle all the way.
Oh! what fun it is to ride
In a one-horse open sleigh. Hey!
Jingle bells, jingle bells,
Jingle all the way;
Oh! what fun it is to ride
In a one-horse open sleigh.

Now the ground is white,
Go it while you're young,
Take the girls tonight
And sing this sleighing song.
Just get a bobtailed bay,
Two forty as his speed,
Hitch him to an open sleigh
And crack! You'll take the lead.

Jingle bells, jingle bells,
Jingle all the way.
Oh! what fun it is to ride
In a one-horse open sleigh. Hey!
Jingle bells, jingle bells,
Jingle all the way;
Oh! what fun it is to ride
In a one-horse open sleigh.

December

Lullabies, Festive Rhymes

1 December • Golden Slumbers Kiss Your Eyes • Thomas Dekker

As the year winds down and the nights draw in, December is a month for lullabies. Our first comes from Thomas Dekker's collaborative play *Patient Grissel* (1603), about a virtuous wife whose legendary endurance shames her bullying husband into repentance. This lovely lyric inspired Paul McCartney's version of 'Golden Slumbers' (1969), which can be found in my book *A Poem for Every Night of the Year*.

Golden slumbers kiss your eyes,
Smiles awake you when you rise.
Sleep, pretty wantons, do not cry,
And I will sing a lullaby:
Rock them, rock them, lullaby.

Care is heavy, therefore sleep you;
You are care, and care must keep you.
Sleep, pretty wantons, do not cry,
And I will sing a lullaby:
Rock them, rock them, lullaby.

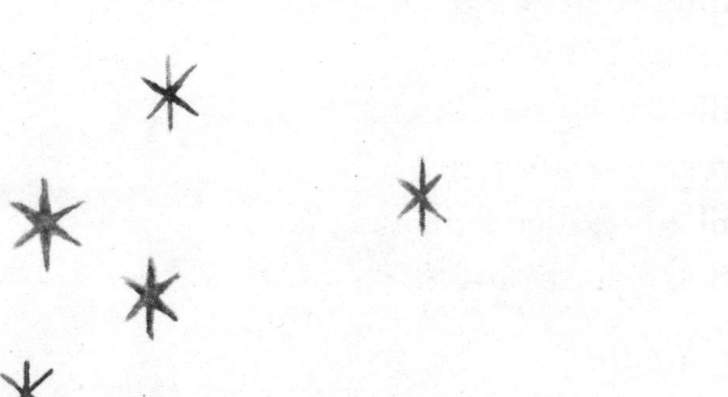

2 December • Wiegenlied (Lullaby) • Johannes Brahms

'Wiegenlied' is an 1868 lullaby; *Lied* is German for song. This one is by the German composer Johannes Brahms (1833–1892), with lyrics from a collection of German folk poems and songs. American heart-throb and singer Frank Sinatra (1915–1998) made a recording of it in 1945.

Lullaby and goodnight,
With roses bedight,
With lilies o'erspread,
'Neath baby's sweet bed.

May thou sleep, may thou rest,
May thy slumber be blest.
May thou sleep, may thou rest,
May thy slumber be blest.

Lullaby and goodnight,
Thy mother's delight.
Bright angels around,
My darling, shall guard.

They will guide thee from harm,
Thou art safe in my arms.
They will guide thee from harm,
Thou art safe in my arms.

3 December • Little Boy Blue • Anon.

Although this lullaby isn't found in any printed material until around 1760, it is thought to be much older. Shakespeare seems to refer to it in his play *King Lear* (1605), when a character pretending to be mad recites the words: 'Sleepest or wakest thou, jolly shepherd? / Thy sheep be in the corn; / And for one blast of thy minikin mouth / Thy sheep shall take no harm.'

Little Boy Blue,
  Come blow your horn,
The sheep's in the meadow
  The cow's in the corn;
Where is that boy
  Who looks after the sheep?
He's under a haystack,
  Fast asleep.
Will you wake him?
  Oh no, not I,
For if I do,
  He'll surely cry.

4 December • Los Pollitos (The Chicks) • Ismael Parraguez

Chilean poet and teacher Ismael Parraguez's *canción de cuna* (lullaby) 'Los Pollitos' ('The Chicks') is sung throughout the Spanish-speaking world. As with Jane Taylor's 'The Star', its popularity has all but rendered it anonymous.

<table>
<tr><td>Los pollitos dicen
Pío, pío, pío
Cuando tienen hambre,
Cuando tienen frio.</td><td>The chicks say
Peep, peep, peep
When they are hungry,
When they are cold.</td></tr>
<tr><td>La gallina busca el maíz
Y el trigo,
Les da la comida y les
Presta abrigo.</td><td>The hen looks for corn
and wheat,
She gives them food
And shelter.</td></tr>
<tr><td>Bajo de sus alas,
Acurrucaditos,
Duermen los pollitos hasta
El otro día.</td><td>Under her wings,
Curled up,
The chicks sleep until
Another day.</td></tr>
<tr><td>*(original)*</td><td>*(translation)*</td></tr>
</table>

5 December • Hush, Little Baby • Anon.

Today's entry might be the most popular lullaby in the English-speaking world, sung by generations of parents to babies at all stages of exhaustion and all hours of the night. During America's folk music revival, the great American singer and Civil Rights activist Nina Simone (1933–2003) covered it for her 1964 album *Folksy Nina*, and more recently the rapper Eminem used lines from the song in his 2005 track 'Mockingbird'.

Hush, little baby, don't say a word,
Mama's gonna buy you a mockingbird.
If that mockingbird don't sing,
Mama's gonna buy you a diamond ring.
If that diamond ring gets broke,
Mama's gonna buy you a billy goat.
If that billy goat won't pull,
Mama's gonna buy you a cart and bull.
If that cart and bull turn over,
Mama's gonna buy you a dog named Rover.
If that dog named Rover won't bark.
Mama's gonna buy you a horse and cart.
If that horse and cart fall down,
You'll still be the sweetest little baby in town.
So hush little baby don't you cry,
'Cause Daddy loves you and so do I.

6 December • Swing Low, Sweet Chariot • Wallace Willis

Like 'Kumbaya' (see 18 January), this song was an African American spiritual which underwent a resurgence during the 1960s folk music revival and Civil Rights struggle. It was written in Oklahoma by Wallace Willis, a Choctaw freedman, some time after the end of the American Civil War in 1865. It has the features of a classic spiritual: call-and-response lyrics, a free-form structure allowing for improvisation, and powerful (possibly coded) Biblical imagery. Its lyrics recall the Old Testament story of the Prophet Elijah going to heaven in a chariot, and a promise of better times ahead. Many have speculated that this song, like 'Follow the Drinking Gourd', was used in the Underground Railroad, particularly due to the lines 'If you get there before I do . . . Tell all my friends I'm coming too'. It is testament to the power of this lyric that the Nazi regime felt the need to ban the song in 1939. More recently, it has been known as an English rugby song.

Swing low, sweet chariot,
Coming for to carry me home.
Swing low, sweet chariot,
Coming for to carry me home.

I looked over Jordan, and what did I see,
Coming for to carry me home?
A band of angels coming after me,
Coming for to carry me home.

Swing low, sweet chariot,
Coming for to carry me home.

Swing low, sweet chariot,
Coming for to carry me home.

If you get there before I do,
Coming for to carry me home.
Tell all my friends I'm coming too,
Coming for to carry me home.

Swing low, sweet chariot,
Coming for to carry me home.
Swing low, sweet chariot,
Coming for to carry me home.

The brightest day that ever I saw,
Coming for to carry me home,
When Jesus washed my sins away,
Coming for to carry me home.

Swing low, sweet chariot,
Coming for to carry me home.
Swing low, sweet chariot,
Coming for to carry me home.

I'm sometimes up and sometimes down,
Coming for to carry me home,
But still my soul feels heaven bound,
Coming for to carry me home.

Swing low, sweet chariot,
Coming for to carry me home.
Swing low, sweet chariot,
Coming for to carry me home.

7 December • Rock-a-Bye, Baby, on the Tree Top • Anon.

There is an edition of *Mother Goose's Melody* dating from around 1765 that features this rhyme, with 'Hush-a-bye' as its opening phrase; most evidence shows that the word 'Rock-a-bye' came along in a later American version. The band Clean Bandit chose to call their 2016 song 'Rockabye', which has had 2.7 billion plays on YouTube alone.

Rock-a-bye, baby, on the tree top,
When the wind blows the cradle will rock;
When the bough breaks the cradle will fall,
Down will come baby, cradle and all.

8 December • Hush-a-Bye, Don't You Cry • Anon.

In 1986, the author Lyn Ellen Lacy developed the theory that this lullaby concerns an enslaved woman forced to give up her own 'poor little baby' to look after the slave owner's child. It later provided the title for American author Cormac McCarthy's bestselling novel *All The Pretty Horses* (1992).

Hush-a-bye, don't you cry,
Go to sleep, my little baby.
When you wake, you shall have
All the pretty little horses.
Black and bays, dapple greys,
Coach and six little horses.

Way down yonder in the meadow
Poor little baby cries 'Mama'
Birds and butterflies flutter round his eyes,
Poor little baby cries 'Mama'.

Hush-a-bye, don't you cry,
Go to sleep, my little baby.
When you wake, you shall have
All the pretty little horses.
Black and bays, dapple greys,
Coach and six little horses.

9 December • Sleep, Baby, Sleep • Anon.

Folklore about magical trees is found in cultures all over the world.

Sleep, baby, sleep,
Thy father guards the sheep;
Thy mother shakes the dreamland tree
And from it fall sweet dreams for thee,
Sleep, baby, sleep.

10 December • Minnie and Winnie • Alfred, Lord Tennyson

Poet Alfred, Lord Tennyson (1809–1892) might be best known for 'The Charge of the Light Brigade', 'The Lady of Shalott' and 'Ulysses', but he also wrote this sweet poem for children.

Minnie and Winnie
Slept in a shell.
Sleep, little ladies!
And they slept well.

Pink was the shell within,
Silver without;
Sounds of the great sea
Wandered about.

Sleep, little ladies,
Wake not soon!
Echo on echo
Dies to the moon.

Two bright stars
Peeped into the shell.
'What are they dreaming of?
Who can tell?'

Started a green linnet
Out of the croft;
Wake, little ladies,
The sun is aloft!

11 December • The Star • Jane Taylor

This poem is so famous and popular that it is often assumed to be by 'Anon.' – though in fact it was written by Jane Taylor (1783–1824) for a book published in collaboration with her sister Ann. The lesser-known verses are included here. Some literary historians consider the Taylor sisters to have been the first English authors to write exclusively for children.

Twinkle, twinkle, little star,
How I wonder what you are!
Up above the world so high,
Like a diamond in the sky.

When the blazing sun is gone,
When he nothing shines upon,
Then you show your little light,
Twinkle, twinkle, all the night.

Then the traveller in the dark,
Thanks you for your tiny spark,
He could not see which way to go,
If you did not twinkle so.

In the dark blue sky you keep,
And often through my curtains peep,
For you never shut your eye,
Till the sun is in the sky.

As your bright and tiny spark,
Lights the traveller in the dark, –
Though I know not what you are,
Twinkle, twinkle, little star.

12 December • Twinkle, Twinkle, Little Bat! • Lewis Carroll

In Lewis Carroll's *Alice's Adventures in Wonderland*, the Mad Hatter delivers this revision of the famous nursery rhyme. It could be a reference to Carroll's friend, the Oxford professor Bartholomew Price, whose nickname was 'The Bat'.

Twinkle, twinkle, little bat!
How I wonder what you're at!
Up above the world you fly,
Like a tea-tray in the sky.
Twinkle, twinkle –
Twinkle, twinkle, twinkle, twinkle.

13 December • My Dreidel • Anon.

Let's pause our run of lullabies before you drop off, and put the light back on for a moment with this popular Hanukkah rhyme. Hanukkah is the eight-day-long Festival of Lights, which commemorates the recovery of Jerusalem and the second temple by the Maccabees, in the second century BC, and starts on the 25th day of the Hebrew month of Kislev – normally between late November and December. A traditional Hanukkah toy is the four-sided spinning top called a dreidel. During the holiday season, spoof Major League Dreidel tournaments are held in New York, in which the player with the longest spin time wins.

I have a little dreidel, I made it out of clay,
And when it's dry and ready, then dreidel I shall play.
Oh, dreidel, dreidel, dreidel, I made it out of clay,
Oh, dreidel, dreidel, dreidel, then dreidel I shall play.

It has a lovely body, with legs so short and thin,
When it gets all tired, it drops and then I win!
Dreidel, dreidel, dreidel, with legs so short and thin,
Oh, dreidel, dreidel, dreidel, it drops and then I win!

My dreidel's always playful, it loves to dance and spin.
A happy game of dreidel, come play now, let's begin.

Oh dreidel, dreidel, dreidel, it loves to dance and spin,
Oh dreidel, dreidel, dreidel, come play now, let's begin.

I have a little dreidel, I made it out of clay,
And when it's dry and ready, then dreidel I shall play.
Oh, dreidel, dreidel, dreidel, I made it out of clay,
Oh, dreidel, dreidel, dreidel, then dreidel I shall play.

14 December • Sweet and Low • Alfred, Lord Tennyson

This is another poem for bedtime by Alfred, Lord Tennyson, extracted from his 1847 poem 'The Princess'.

Sweet and low, sweet and low,
    Wind of the western sea,
Low, low, breathe and blow,
    Wind of the western sea!
Over the rolling waters go,
Come from the dying moon, and blow,
    Blow him again to me;
While my little one, while my pretty one, sleeps.

Sleep and rest, sleep and rest,
    Father will come to thee soon;
Rest, rest, on mother's breast,
    Father will come to thee soon;
Father will come to his babe in the nest,
Silver sails all out of the west
    Under the silver moon:
Sleep, my little one, sleep, my pretty one, sleep.

15 December • Baby's Bed's a Silver Moon • Anon.

Now begins a run of bedtime rhymes with sailing as their theme.

Baby's bed's a silver moon
    Sailing o'er the sky,
Sailing o'er the sea of sleep,
    While the stars go by.

Sail, baby, sail,
    Far across the sea.
And don't forget to come
    Back home again to me.

Baby's fishing for a dream,
    Fishing near and far,
Her line a silver moonbeam is,
    Her bait a silver star.

Sail, baby, sail,
    Far across the sea.
But don't forget to come
    Back home again to me.

16 December • My Bed is a Boat • Robert Louis Stevenson

Robert Louis Stevenson's childhood nurse, Alison Cunningham, to whom his collection of children's poetry was dedicated, is briefly mentioned here. It would be far easier to sleep in this ship than the one manned by Long John Silver in Stevenson's pirate adventure *Treasure Island* (1883).

My bed is like a little boat;
    Nurse helps me in when I embark;
She girds me in my sailor's coat
    And starts me in the dark.

At night I go on board and say
    Good-night to all my friends on shore;
I shut my eyes and sail away
    And see and hear no more.

And sometimes things to bed I take,
    As prudent sailors have to do;
Perhaps a slice of wedding-cake,
    Perhaps a toy or two.

All night across the dark we steer;
    But when the day returns at last,
Safe in my room, beside the pier,
    I find my vessel fast.

17 December • Wynken, Blynken and Nod • Eugene Field

The 'wooden shoe', 'herring-fish' and the characters' names sound Dutch in this poem by Eugene Field (1850–1895), which was indeed originally called 'Dutch Lullaby'.

Wynken, Blynken, and Nod one night
    Sailed off in a wooden shoe, –
Sailed on a river of crystal light
    Into a sea of dew.
'Where are you going, and what do you wish?'
    The old moon asked the three.
'We have come to fish for the herring-fish
    That live in this beautiful sea;
    Nets of silver and gold have we,'
        Said Wynken,
        Blynken,
        And Nod.

The old moon laughed and sang a song,
    As they rocked in the wooden shoe;
And the wind that sped them all night long
    Ruffled the waves of dew;
The little stars were the herring-fish
    That lived in the beautiful sea.
'Now cast your nets wherever you wish, –
    Never afraid are we!'
    So cried the stars to the fishermen three,
        Wynken,
        Blynken,
        And Nod.

All night long their nets they threw
To the stars in the twinkling foam, –
Then down from the skies came the wooden shoe,
Bringing the fishermen home:
'Twas all so pretty a sail, it seemed
As if it could not be;
And some folk thought 'twas a dream they'd dreamed
Of sailing that beautiful sea;
But I shall name you the fishermen three:
Wynken,
Blynken,
And Nod.

Wynken and Blynken are two little eyes,
And Nod is a little head,
And the wooden shoe that sailed the skies
Is a wee one's trundle-bed;
So shut your eyes while Mother sings
Of wonderful sights that be,
And you shall see the beautiful things
As you rock in the misty sea
Where the old shoe rocked the fishermen three: –
Wynken,
Blynken,
And Nod.

18 December • The Land of Nod • Robert Louis Stevenson

This bedtime poem is from Robert Louis Stevenson's collection *A Child's Garden of Verses* (1885). 'The land of Nod' is a biblical allusion to where Cain ends up after his wandering: 'And Cain went out from the presence of the Lord, and dwelt in the land of Nod, on the east of Eden' (Genesis 4:18-16).

From breakfast on through all the day
At home among my friends I stay,
But every night I go abroad
Afar into the land of Nod.

All by myself I have to go,
With none to tell me what to do –
All alone beside the streams
And up the mountain-sides of dreams.

The strangest things are there for me,
Both things to eat and things to see,
And many frightening sights abroad
Till morning in the land of Nod.

Try as I like to find the way,
I never can get back by day,
Nor can remember plain and clear
The curious music that I hear.

19 December • Christmas is Coming • Anon.

Wake up, it's nearly Christmas! The festive period was the time of year when beggars could expect to be met with generosity. Before the twentieth century, goose was Britain's traditional Christmas bird.

> Christmas is coming.
> The geese are getting fat.
> Please to put a penny in the old man's hat.
> If you haven't got a penny,
> A ha'penny will do.
> If you haven't got a ha'penny
> Then God bless you.

20 December • We Wish You a Merry Christmas • Anon.

'Figgy pudding' is a traditional English steamed pudding. Here's a simple recipe: Mix 225g chopped dried figs, 110g flour, 110g suet, 110g sugar, 1 tsp baking powder, a pinch of salt and a pinch of ground nutmeg. Beat 210ml milk and 2 eggs in a jug, then stir into mixture. Pour mixture into pudding basin and steam for 2.5 hours in a pan of boiling water, reaching halfway up the pudding basin. Serves 8.

We wish you a merry Christmas,
We wish you a merry Christmas,
We wish you a merry Christmas,
and a happy new year!

Good tidings we bring to you and your kin,
We wish you a merry Christmas and a happy new year!

Now bring us some figgy pudding,
Now bring us some figgy pudding,
Now bring us some figgy pudding,
And bring some out here!

Good tidings we bring to you and your kin
We wish you a merry Christmas and a happy new year!

For we all like figgy pudding,
We all like figgy pudding,
We all like figgy pudding,
So bring some out here!

Good tidings we bring to you and your kin,
We wish you a merry Christmas and a happy new year!

And we won't go until we've got some,
We won't go until we've got some,
We won't go until we've got some,
So bring some out here!

Good tidings we bring to you and your kin,
We wish you a merry Christmas and a
happy new year!

21 December • Old King Cole • Anon.

This festive rhyme first appeared in the early eighteenth century. The great writer Sir Walter Scott (1771–1832) – of *Rob Roy* fame – suggested that Old King Cole might be the father of Ireland's mythological giant Fionn mac Cumhaill – pronounced Finn McCool.

Old King Cole
Was a merry old soul,
And a merry old soul was he;
He called for his pipe,
And he called for his bowl,
And he called for his fiddlers three.

Now every fiddler, he had a fiddle,
And a very fine fiddle had he;
Twee tweedle dee, tweedle dee, went the fiddlers.
Oh, there's none so rare
As can compare
With King Cole and his fiddlers three!

22 December • Deck the Halls • Anon.

It's time to decorate your house for the holidays, says this traditional carol.

Deck the halls with boughs of holly,
Fa, la, la, la, la, la, la, la, la!
'Tis the season to be jolly,
Fa, la, la, la, la, la, la, la, la!
Don we now our gay apparel,
Fa, la, la, la, la, la, la, la, la!
Troll the ancient Yuletide carol.
Fa, la, la, la, la, la, la, la, la!

See the blazing Yule before us.
Fa, la, la, la, la, la, la, la, la!
Strike the harp and join the chorus,
Fa, la, la, la, la, la, la, la, la!
Follow me in merry measure,
Fa, la, la, la, la, la, la, la, la!
While I tell of Yuletide treasure.
Fa, la, la, la, la, la, la, la, la!

Fast away the old year passes,
Fa, la, la, la, la, la, la, la, la!
Hail the new, ye lads and lasses,
Fa, la, la, la, la, la, la, la, la!
Sing we joyous all together,
Fa, la, la, la, la, la, la, la, la!
Heedless of the wind and weather.
Fa, la, la, la, la, la, la, la, la!

23 December • Little Jack Horner • Anon.

There's a legend of skulduggery attached to this festive rhyme. The original 'Jack Horner' might be one Thomas Horner, who was a steward to Abbot Whiting, of Glastonbury. At the time of the Dissolution of the Monasteries, Whiting sent Horner to take a pie to Henry VIII. On his way to the King, it is said that Horner cut open the pie and found the deeds of the Manor of Mells hidden inside. Records show that Horner was a member of the jury who condemned Abbot Whiting to his death, and that for hundreds of years the Horner family lived at Mells.

Little Jack Horner
Sat in the corner,
Eating a Christmas pie;
He put in his thumb,
And pulled out a plum,
And said, 'What a good boy am I!'

24 December • On Christmas Eve I Turned the Spit • Anon.

This was originally part of a seasonal mummers' play. Mummers' plays are British folk plays, performed by informal troupes of amateur actors – not plays in which the actors are barely audible!

> On Christmas Eve I turned the spit,
> I burnt my fingers, I feel it yet;
> The cock sparrow flew over the table,
> The pot began to play with the ladle;
> The ladle stood up like a naked man,
> And vowed he'd fight the frying-pan;
> The frying-pan behind the door
> Said he never saw the like before;
> And the kitchen clock I was going to wind
> Said he never saw the like behind.

25 December • The Twelve Days of Christmas • Anon.

This famous cumulative rhyme, possibly originating in France, is accompanied by a game in the North of England where forgetting the last line results in a penalty. Imagine the amount of wrapping paper the true love would get through on the drummers alone!

On the first day of Christmas, my true love gave to me
A partridge in a pear tree.

On the second day of Christmas, my true love gave to me
Two turtle doves
And a partridge in a pear tree.

On the third day of Christmas, my true love gave to me
Three French hens,
Two turtle doves
And a partridge in a pear tree.

On the fourth day of Christmas, my true love gave to me
Four calling birds,
Three French hens,
Two turtle doves
And a partridge in a pear tree.

On the fifth day of Christmas, my true love gave to me
Five gold rings,
Four calling birds,
Three French hens,
Two turtle doves
And a partridge in a pear tree.

On the sixth day of Christmas, my true love gave to me
Six geese a-laying,
Five gold rings,
Four calling birds,
Three French hens,
Two turtle doves
And a partridge in a pear tree.

On the seventh day of Christmas, my true love gave to me
Seven swans a-swimming,
Six geese a-laying,
Five gold rings,
Four calling birds,
Three French hens,
Two turtle doves
And a partridge in a pear tree.

On the eighth day of Christmas, my true love gave to me
Eight maids a-milking,
Seven swans a-swimming,
Six geese a-laying,
Five gold rings,
Four calling birds,
Three French hens,
Two turtle doves
And a partridge in a pear tree.

On the ninth day of Christmas, my true love gave to me
Nine ladies dancing,
Eight maids a-milking,
Seven swans a-swimming,
Six geese a-laying,

Five gold rings,
Four calling birds,
Three French hens,
Two turtle doves
And a partridge in a pear tree.

On the tenth day of Christmas, my true love gave to me
Ten lords a-leaping,
Nine ladies dancing,
Eight maids a-milking,
Seven swans a-swimming,
Six geese a-laying,
Five gold rings,
Four calling birds,
Three French hens,
Two turtle doves
And a partridge in a pear tree.

On the eleventh day of Christmas, my true love gave to me
Eleven pipers piping,
Ten lords a-leaping,
Nine ladies dancing,
Eight maids a-milking,
Seven swans a-swimming,
Six geese a-laying,
Five gold rings,
Four calling birds,
Three French hens,
Two turtle doves
And a partridge in a pear tree.

On the twelfth day of Christmas, my true love gave to me
Twelve drummers drumming,
Eleven pipers piping,
Ten lords a-leaping,
Nine ladies dancing,
Eight maids a-milking,
Seven swans a-swimming,
Six geese a-laying,
Five gold rings,
Four calling birds,
Three French hens,
Two turtle doves,
And a partridge in a pear tree.

26 December • Good King Wenceslas • John Mason Neale

The Feast of St Stephen is the second day of Christmas, more often known as Boxing Day. This 1853 carol is by the English hymn writer John Mason Neale (1818–1866), and tells of Saint Wenceslaus I, Duke of Bohemia (907–935) going out to give alms to a poor peasant. Though only a duke in his lifetime, he was considered a saint after his death and Holy Roman Emperor Otto I (962–973) posthumously conferred on him the title 'King'.

Good King Wencelas looked out
    On the Feast of Stephen,
When the snow lay round about,
    Deep, and crisp, and even;
Brightly shone the moon that night,
    Though the frost was cruel,
When a poor man came in sight,
    Gath'ring winter fuel.

'Hither, page, and stand by me,
    If thou know'st it, telling,
Yonder peasant, who is he?
    Where and what is his dwelling?'
'Sire, he lives a good league hence.
    Underneath the mountain;
Right against the forest fence,
    By Saint Agnes' fountain.'

'Bring me flesh, and bring me wine,
  Bring me pine-logs hither:
Thou and I will see him dine,
  When we bear them thither.'
Page monarch forth they went,
  Forth they went together;
Through the rude wind's wild lament,
  And the bitter weather.

'Sire, the night is darker now,
  And the wind blows stronger;
Fails my heart, I know now how,
  I can go no longer.'
'Mark my footsteps, good my page;
  Tread thou in them boldly;
Thou shalt find the winter's rage
  Freeze thy blood less coldly.'

In his master's steps he trod,
  Where the snow lay dinted
Heat was in the very sod
  Which the Saint had printed.
Therefore, Christian men, be sure,
  Wealth or rank possessing,
Ye, who now will bless the poor,
  Shall yourselves find blessing.

27 December • Jack-a-Nory • Anon.

This is a rhyme traditionally used to put off children's demands for a story. Its leading character gave its name to the BBC children's programme *Jackanory*.

I'll tell you a story
About Jack-a-Nory,
And now my story's begun;
I'll tell you another,
About Jack and his brother,
And now my story is done.

28 December • Each Peach Pear Plum • Anon.

This traditional rhyme, which delightfully recaps some of the characters we have met throughout the year, inspired a wildly successful children's book of the same name, by Janet and Allan Ahlberg.

Each peach pear plum
I spy Tom Thumb.

Tom Thumb fast asleep
I spy Bo-Peep.

Bo-Peep round the corner
I spy Jack Horner.

Jack Horner up a pole
I spy King Cole.

King Cole drinking juice
I spy Mother Goose.

Mother Goose told a story
I spy Jackanory.

29 December • At the End of the Day • Anon.

This pious rhyme is sometimes recited – with varying degrees of honesty – at the end of the day in English primary schools.

At the end of the day, just kneel and say:
'Thank you, Lord, for my work and play;
I've tried to be good, for I know that I should.'
That's a prayer for the end of the day!

30 December • A Wee Bird Sat upon a Tree • Anon.

From the end of the day to the end of the year: this sweet Scottish rhyme is likely about the brambling, one of the smallest species of winter birds.

A wee bird sat upon a tree,
When the year was done and auld,
And aye it cheeped so piteously,
'My, but it's cold, cold!'

31 December • Girls and Boys, Come out to Play • Anon.

Our final rhyme for the year celebrates the thrill of staying up late to celebrate. Happy New Year's Eve!

Girls and boys, come out to play,
The moon doth shine as bright as day.
Leave your supper, and leave your sleep,
And come with your playfellows into the street.
Come with a whoop, come with a call,
Come with good will, or come not at all.
Up the ladder and down the wall,
A halfpenny loaf will serve us all.
You find milk, and I'll find flour,
And we'll have a pudding in half an hour.

Sources and Further Reading

Books:

Acorn Nursery School Songbook

Ada, Alma Flor and Campoy, F. Isabel, *Muu, Moo! Rimas de Animales/Animal Nursery Rhymes: Bilingual Spanish–English* (London: Harper Collins, 2010)

Bacon, Paul, *The Frank Loesser Songbook* (New York: Simon and Schuster, 1971)

Baker, Richard Anthony, *British Music Hall: An Illustrated History* (Cheltenham: The History Press, 2014)

Baring-Gould, William S. and Baring-Gould, Cecil, *The Annotated Mother Goose: Nursery Rhymes Old and New, Arranged and Explained* (Devon: Bramhall House, 1962)

Baring-Gould, William, *The Lure of the Limerick* (London: Panther Books, 1970)

Benjamin, Floella, *Skip Across the Ocean: Nursery rhymes from around the world* (London, Frances Lincoln Children's Books, 2007)

Blishen, Edward, *Oxford Book of Poetry for Children* (Oxford: Oxford University Press, 1963)

Colquhoun, Neil, *Song of a young country: An Anthology of New Zealand Folk Music* (Michigan: Bailey Brothers, 1973)

Comer, Karen, *The Children's Illustrated Treasury of Nursery Rhymes* (Victoria: Hinkler, 2015)

Corbett, Pie, *The Works Key Stage 1: Poems and Rhymes to Enjoy, Read, Perform and Learn by Heart* (London: Macmillan, 2006)

Cryer, Max, *Love Me Tender: The Stories Behind The World's Best-Loved Songs* (London: Frances Lincoln, 2008)

Delamar, Gloria T. *Mother Goose: From Nursery to Literature* (Jefferson: McFarland & Co, 1987)

DePaola, Tomie, *Tomie DePaola's Mother Goose* (London: Methuen Children, 1985)

Dutta, Sanji, *Hindi Nursery Rhymes 1* (London: Mantra Publishing, 1988)

Faustin, Charles, *The Kiskadee Queen: A Collection of Black Nursery Verse* (London: Puffin, 1991)

Foss, Michael, *A Treasury of Nursery Rhymes* (London: Michael O'Mara Books, 1985)

Fyleman, Rose, *Widdy-widdy-wurkey* (London: Basil Blackwell, 1936)

Greenaway, Kate, *Nursery Rhyme Classics* (London: Leopard, 1995)

Hall, Donald, *The Oxford Book of Children's Verse in America* (Oxford: Oxford University Press, 1985)

Hammill, Elizabeth, *Over the Hills and Far Away* (London: Frances Lincoln Books, 2014)

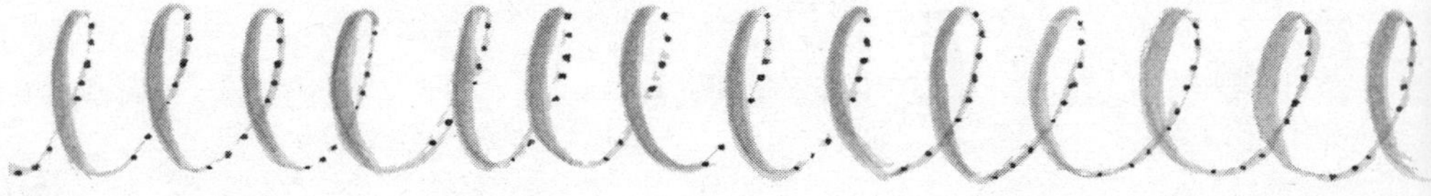

Henderson, Kathy and Smy, Pam, *Hush, Baby, Hush! Lullabies from Around the World* (London: Frances Lincoln Children's Books, 2010)

Ireson, Barbara, *The Faber Book of Nursery Verse* (London: Faber, 1983)

Jack, Albert, *Pop Goes the Weasel: The Secret Meanings of Nursery Rhymes* (London: Penguin, 2010)

Jerrold, Walter, *Mother Goose's Nursery Rhymes* (London: Random House, 2003)

Kipling, Rudyard, *Just So Stories* (London: Tobar, 2008)

Marks, Anthony, *The Usborne Children's Songbook* (London: Usborne, 1988)

Mayo, Margaret, *If You Should Meet a Crocodile and other verse* (London: Kaye & Ward, 1974)

Milne, A.A., *When We Were Very Young* (London: Egmont, 2016)

Mitchell, Donald and Blyton, Carey, *The Faber Book of Nursery Songs* (London: Faber, 1968)

Mitchell, Donald, *Every Child's Book of Nursery Songs* (New York: Crown, 1985)

Montgomerie, Norah and Montgomerie, William, *Scottish Nursery Rhymes* (London: The Hogarth Press, 1975)

Moorat, Joseph, *Nursery Songs 1912* (London: Thames and Hudson, 1980)

Morgan, Gaby, *Poems of Childhood* (London, Macmillan, 2019)

Morris, Jackie, *The Jackie Morris Book of Classic Nursery Rhymes* (Herefordshire, Otter-Barry, 2020)

Mulherin, Jennifer, *Popular Nursery Rhymes* (London: Collins, 1981)

Opie, Iona and Opie, Peter, *Children's Games in Street and Playground* (Edinburgh, Floris Books, 1969)

Opie, Iona and Opie, Peter, *The Oxford Dictionary of Nursery Rhymes* (Oxford: Oxford University Press, 1995)

Piwan, Hema, *Gujarati Nursery Rhymes* (London: Mantra Publishing, 1988)

Potter, Beatrix, *Appley Dapply's Nursery Rhymes* (London: F. Warner, 1917)

Prelutsky, Jack, *The Walker Book of Read-Aloud Rhymes for the Very Young* (London: Walker Books Ltd, 1988)

Rackham, Arthur, *Mother Goose Nursery Rhymes* [1913] (London: Chancellor Press, 1985)

Rosen, Michael, *A World of Poetry* (London: Kingfisher, 1991)

Rosen, Michael, *Honey for You, Honey for Me* (London: Walker Books, 2020)

Rosen, Michael, *Michael Rosen's Book of Nonsense* (Hove: Macdonald Young Books, 1997)

Sandburg, Charles, *The American Songbag* (London: Harcourt Brace and Company, 1927)

Schenk De Regniers, Beatrice, *Poems children will sit still for; a selection for the*

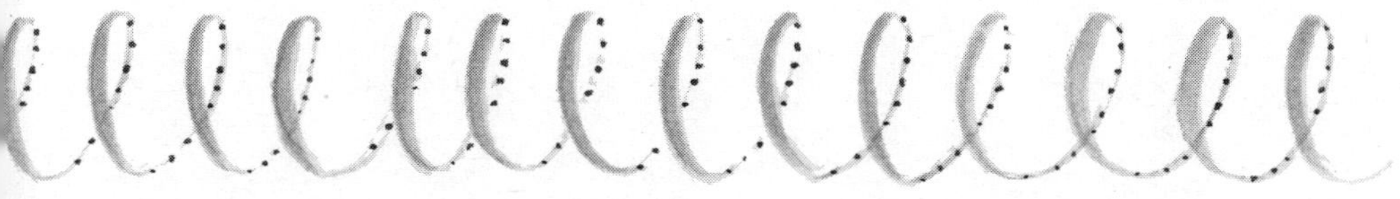

primary grades (New York: Citation Press, 1969)

Smith, E. Boyd, *The Boyd Smith Mother Goose* (New York: G. P. Putnam's Sons, 1920)

Spriggs, Ruth, *Frank Baber's Mother Goose Nursery Rhymes* (London: Peter Lowe, 1988)

Stanford, C.V., *The National Song Book: A Complete Collection of the Folk-Songs, Carols, and Rounds Suggested by the Board of Education* (London: Creative Media Partners, LLC 1905)

Stevenson, Robert Louis, *A Child's Garden of Verses* (London: Simon & Schuster, 1999)

Talley, Thomas W., *Negro Folk Rhymes Wise and Otherwise: With a Study* (New York: Macmillan, 1922)

Taylor, Alice, *A Child's Book of Irish Rhymes* (London: Gill & Macmillan, 1996)

Thompson, Carol, *Bedtime Rhymes* (London: Orchard Books, 1997)

Tucker, Nicholas, *Mother Goose Abroad* (London: Hamish Hamilton, 1974)

Uzo Unobagha, *Off to the Sweet Shores of Africa: And Other Talking Drum Rhymes* (San Francisco: Chronicle Books, 2000)

Waters, Fiona, *Tiger, Tiger, Burning Bright: An Animal Poem for Every Day of the Year* (Nosy Crow: London, 2020)

Webb, Sarah and Ranson, Claire, *Sally Go Round the Stars: Favourite Rhymes from an Irish Childhood* (Dublin: The O'Brien Press, 2011)

Wells, Carolyn, *A Nonsense Anthology* (New York: Charles Scribner's Sons, 1903)

Yolen, Jane, *Street Rhymes Around the World* (Toledo: Discover Books, 2000)

Websites consulted include:

Academy of American Poets, https://www.poets.org

BBC Teach, https://www.bbc.co.uk/teach/school-radio/

Poetry Foundation, https://poetryfoundation.org

Scottish Poetry Library, https://www.scottishpoetrylibrary.org.uk/

Journals consulted include:

Worthington, Mabel P., 'Nursery Rhymes in Finnegans Wake' in *The Journal of American Folklore*, vol. 70, no. 275 (pp. 37–48).

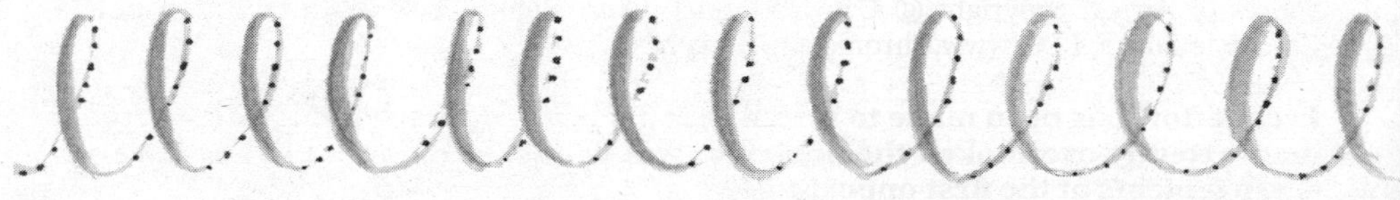

The compiler and publisher would like to thank the following for permission to use their copyright material:

Agard, John: 'Don't Call Alligator Long-Mouth till You Cross the River' copyright © John Agard 1986 reproduced by kind permission of John Agard c/o Caroline Sheldon Literary Agency Ltd; **Andreae, Giles:** 'My Sister', copyright © Giles Andreae. Reproduced with kind permission of the author; **Benjamin, Floella:** 'Lock In, Lock Up, All Lock Down'. Reprinted by kind permission of the author; **Bentley, E. C.:** 'Sir Christopher Wren', copyright © 1905. Reproduced with permission of Curtis Brown Ltd, London, on behalf of the Estate of E. Clerihew Bentley; **Bevan, Clare:** 'If You Hear', 'A Bedtime Rhyme for Young Fairies' and 'Mermaid School'. Reprinted by kind permission of the author; **Bilston, Brian:** 'Rain, Will You Come Today', '1-2-3-4' and 'Remember, Remember'. Copyright © Brian Bilston. Reprinted by permission of Jo Unwin Literary Agency; **Butler, Ralph and Hart, Peter:** Lyrics 'Nellie The Elephant', Words and Music by Ralph Butler and Peter Hart. Copyright © 1956 Dash Music Co. Ltd. Copyright Renewed. All Rights Reserved. Used by Permission. Reprinted by Permission of Hal Leonard Europe Ltd; **Campbell, Rod:** 'At Playschool', 'Creepy Crawlies', 'Toy Train' first published in *Lift-the-Flap Nursery Book* (Macmillan, 1993). Reprinted by kind permission of the author; **Coelho, Joseph:** 'Blow a Kiss' Copyright © Joseph Coelho, 2022. Published with permission from Andersen Press Ltd; **Donaldson, Julia:** 'Noisy Garden' from *Crazy Mayonnaisy Mum* copyright © Julia Donaldson 2004 and 'One More Story' copyright © Julia Donaldson 2021 reproduced by kind permission of Julia Donaldson c/o Caroline Sheldon Literary Agency Ltd; **Halls, Smriti:** 'Chillies are Red' reprinted by kind permission of the author; **Hamilton, Arthur:** Lyrics 'Sing A Rainbow' Words and Music by Arthur Hamilton. Copyright © 1955 (Renewed) Mark VII Ltd, Warner Chappell North America Ltd, London, W8 5DA. Reproduced by permission of Faber Music Ltd. All Rights Reserved; **Hammerstein II, Oscar:** Lyrics 'Do-Re-Mi' from *The Sound of Music*. Lyrics by Oscar Hammerstein II. Music by Richard Rodgers. Copyright © 1959 Williamson Music Company c/o Concord Music Publishing. Copyright Renewed. All Rights Reserved. Used by Permission. Reprinted by Permission of Hal Leonard Europe Ltd; **Kelley, Clarence Z. and Sanders, George:** Lyrics 'I'm A Little Teapot' Words and music by Clarence Z. Kelley and George Sanders Copyright © 1939. All Rights Reserved. Reprinted by permission of Marilyn Sanders Music LLC; **Lipton, Leonard and Yarrow, Peter:** Lyrics: 'Puff The Magic Dragon' Words and Music by Peter Yarrow and Leonard Lipton. Copyright © 1963 (Renewed 1991) Silver Dawn Music and Honalee Melodies. All Rights for Silver Dawn Music Administered by Warner Chappell North America Ltd., London, W8 5DA (70%). All Rights for Honalee Melodies Administered by BMG Rights Management (US) LLC (30%). Reproduced by permission of Faber Music Ltd; and Hal Leonard Europe Ltd. All Rights Reserved; **Loesser, Frank:** Lyrics 'The Ugly Duckling' from the Motion Picture Hans Christian Andersen by Frank Loesser. Copyright © 1951, 1952 (Renewed) Frank Music Corp. All Rights Reserved. Reprinted by Permission of Hal Leonard Europe Ltd; **Milligan, Spike:** 'On the Ning Nang Nong'. Reproduced by kind permission of Spike Milligan Productions Limited; **Milne, A. A.:** 'Vespers' and 'The King's Breakfast' from *When We Were Very Young*, copyright © Pooh Properties Trust 1924. Reproduced with permission of HarperCollins Publishers and Curtis Brown Group Ltd on behalf of The Pooh Properties Trust; **Rosen, Michael:** 'Beans' and 'A Man With An Enormous Nose' from *Michael Rosen's Book of Nonsense* reprinted by permission of Peters Fraser & Dunlop (www.petersfraserdunlop.com) on behalf of Michael Rosen; **Unobagha, Uzo:** 'Ramadan! Hamadan! Here I come!' and 'On the muddy bank of the Zambezi' from *Off to the Sweet Shores of Africa*, copyright © Uzo Unobagha 2000. Reproduced with permission from Chronicle Books, LLC, www.ChronicleBooks.com.

Every effort has been made to trace the copyright holders, but if any have been inadvertently overlooked the publisher will be pleased to make the necessary arrangements at the first opportunity.

Index of First Lines

Index of Names and Themes

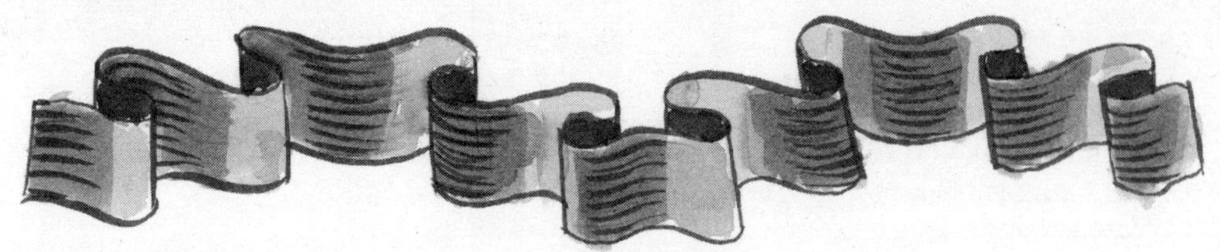

With huge thanks to

The team at Macmillan – Gaby Morgan, Jo Hardacre, Camilla Leask, Sarah Plows, Sarah Ramsey, Tracey Ridgewell, Rachel Vale, Louisa Cusworth, Charlie Castelletti, Emily Jones, Farzana Khan, researcher Stevie Doran, Nick de Somogyi, the National Poetry Library, and all my friends who have been singing me nursery rhymes from their childhoods.

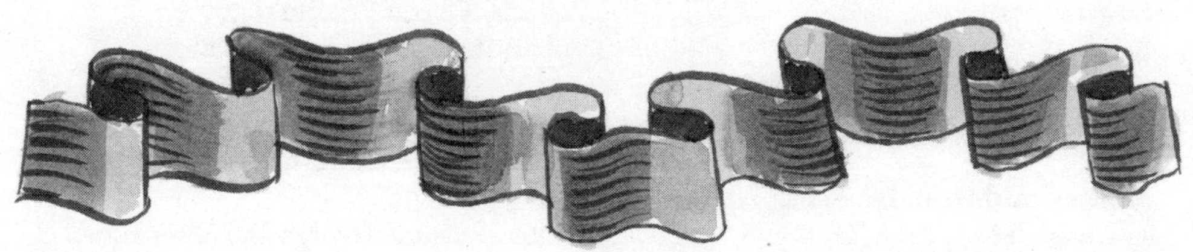